SAMUEL LITTLE AND OTHER TALES OF TRUE CRIME

LARRY MARAVICH

TABLE OF CONTENTS
SAMUEL LITTLE
FOOTPATH MURDERER
KILLER DOCTOR
GRANNY KILLER
PATRICIA MEEHAN
KELSIE SCHELLING
NATALEE HOLLOWAY
JENNIFER KESSE
TARA CALICO

Making a Murderer

When the ingredients of a recipe are mixed together, and put on the hob to boil, different flavours bubble to the surface. The horror filled dish that is Samuel Little has only recently – in November of 2018, in fact – started to reveal its full range of unpleasant attacks on our senses.

The essence of what is starting to emerge may well change over the coming weeks and months; it might get stronger and even less palatable, it may turn out to be a false concoction which, with investigation, proves to still contain a bitter taste. One still unbelievably bad to those who have had the misfortune to find it on their plate, but (at least) something about which we already know.

Because, if there is even a fraction of truth in what Samuel Little is currently saying, the United States is about to know the identity of its latest, biggest ever, serial killer.

Those ingredients which created this man, now aging away serving a life sentence in a prison cell, are classics of the criminal fraternity. From the outset, he was someone who had little chance to make it good. Not that this is any kind of excuse for the crimes we already know Samuel Little has committed, nor for the overwhelming number which he has claimed to have perpetrated beyond those confirmed atrocities. Many people grow up in difficult circumstances, find their life chances limited by factors outside of their control, and overcome these to turn into valued and important members of society. Nevertheless Little's background is one which has 'future career criminal' plastered all over it, like an allergy warning on a packet of mixed nuts.

He was born just prior to the US entry into the second world war, in the tiny southern town of Reynolds, Georgia. The black population here might have outnumbered the white, but there could be no doubt where the balance of power lay. This was a time, in the South, of widespread segregation and open discrimination. Indeed, the 'Jim Crow' laws still held sway. Effectively discrimination was not only a part of life, but deemed constitutional; segregation was regarded as a proper state of affairs. Certainly, when blacks began fighting alongside whites in the war the slow process towards change began, but that was too far in the future for the infant Little and his family.

There was nothing for them in Georgia, and quite early in his life, Little was moved north to Lorain, Ohio. Unfortunately, though, the seeds of a life had been laid, and to the twin disadvantages of racial discrimination and poverty was added a liberal dose of poor parenting. Still, while there might be less ingrained prejudice in this city on the banks of Lake Erie than there was in Georgia during the 1940s, it was hardly paradise. A rough, tough industrial centre, known for shipbuilding, the city had more than its own fair share of poverty. While it couldn't match the levels of destitution of nearby Cleveland, it was still a place where impoverishment was considerably above the national average.

For a young black child growing up there against a backdrop of war, there was nothing. Opportunity, education, later jobs – the prospects for each of these were exceptionally poor. His situation was not helped when Little's parents disappeared off the scene, and he was largely brought up by his grandmother.

It was of no surprise that Little quickly began to fail in his education, and did not complete High School. Those who have interviewed him confirm that he is blessed with intelligence and a calming presence, but these did not translate to educational success. Still, it is easy to believe how, later in life, he could convince women that they were safe with him, make them relax their guard. Much later, but by the time began his killing spree, he had acquired yet another ingredient to his make-up. He learned to box, and employed that skill to render his victims helpless.

Still, that was a way ahead. He was just fifteen years old when apprehended for the first time. By then he was on his own, and was living in Nebraska. There, he was arrested for burglary in Omaha, and served time in a youth penitentiary. A place where, no doubt, he perfected his nefarious skills, listening to and learning from those with more experience of delinquent activity.

He learned a lot, and became an expert criminal in his own right. Over the following twenty years, Little was arrested no less than twenty six times. Sometimes he used the alias Samuel McDowell, but whether operating under this or his real name, Little's expertise lay not so much in not getting caught, but in avoiding prison. Although he was arrested for, among other offences, shoplifting, rape, aggravated assault, attacking a police officer, theft, driving under the influence, breaking and entering, fraud and even solicitation of a prostitute, rarely did he find himself behind bars. It seems in hindsight astonishing that such a career criminal could avoid rehabilitation or, often, punishment. In many ways, this is yet another contribution society made to creating the killer, or at least the circumstances in which he could operate.

However, it was during one of his rare forays into a spell under lock and key that he learned to box. Later, police would discover that often his mode of operation was to punch his victims, rendering them unconscious, before sexually assaulting, raping and, often it seems, murdering them.

Perhaps one of the reasons he managed to avoid jail was that Little was a transient criminal. He was frequently homeless; he lived out of his car, from which he sold stolen goods to dope dealers and others from the underworld.

Over a twenty year spell starting from his release from youth detention in 1957, he found himself arrested in no less than eleven states. These were his home state of Georgia, and his adopted one of Ohio. In addition he came to police attention in Maryland, Florida, Arizona and California. Massachusetts, Oregon, Philadelphia, Illinois and New Jersey also proved to be centres for his criminal activities.

So, the recipe was almost complete: Little was born into a poor world filled with prejudice; he was moved out of his home environment to a new one thousands of miles away from his early years; his parents disappeared out of his life; he failed at school; he possessed the intelligence and charm to inveigle his way into people's trust but not the compassion to utilise that for good; he developed the skills of a criminal in the best school possible – a youth detention centre; he practised and perfected those skills over a twenty year period, across the entire country. And when caught – which he often was – society failed to either properly punish or work with him towards rehabilitation. But he was an uneducated black man in this embarrassing era of American History – he was disregarded, like household rubbish. When that rubbish is thrown back out onto the streets, it rots, and ferments, and causes harm to others.

In 1975 Little was back in the state of his birth, Georgia. He was arrested by the Macon police department for Driving Under Influence; the mug shot shows a man of his time; big afro hair, snappy blue suit, wide labelled multi patterned shirt, neatly clipped moustache and beard. He could almost have been a TV star of his day. As he was charged for drunk driving, he gave his name as William Lewis. What the

Macon police did not know was that not only was his name not William Lewis, but the man before them had already moved from petty and mid-level crime to murder.

It would be another eight years, however, before police began to suspect that Little could be the perpetrator of a number of killings.

In 2012 Little was once more in trouble with the authorities. He had been arrested in Kentucky on drug related charges, and the developing national crime database threw up something of interest to some cold case investigators in the LAPD. The matters reached the attention of Detectives Mitzi Roberts and Rick Jackson.

They discovered DNA evidence linking Little to three murders carried out in the late 1980s. The streets of Los Angeles were a dangerous place for women in that time. The 'Grim Sleeper', Lonnie David Franklin Jr, was at the height of his attacks. The city was unsafe, particularly for women plying their trade in the sex industry, and one of the biggest threats came from Samuel Little. Carol Alford was 41 when she was murdered in 1987, Audrey Nelson (35) and Guadalupe Apodaca (46) were killed in 1989.

The three had murders had a couple of things in common. The victims were all strangled; all were dumped in back alleys with no real attempt to hide them and on each was found the DNA of the same person.

Roberts and Jackson identified that DNA as belonging to Samuel Little. It soon became apparent, from checking records of the time, that in the late 80s the man in question was living in the Los Angeles and San Diego areas, and was widely involved in all kinds of crime. Further, he had just been paroled from one of his rare spells behind bars.

'It was theft by day and murder by night,' said Jackson.

But there was still not enough evidence to arrest Little for the murders. Back in the 1980s, the use of DNA evidence was very much in its infancy, and matters such as collection and storage were nothing like at the standards they are today. More evidence would be needed. However, for Detective Roberts, it soon became apparent that they could have an even more widespread serial killer on their hands.

'We believe he is good for many more crimes – including murders – throughout the United States. If any law enforcement agencies have similar killings that occurred between 1960 and the present, they should contact LAPD Cold Case Detectives,' said the officer back in 2012.

But as the case around Little grew, he proved to suddenly be a difficult man to trace. Then, Louisiana deputies found evidence of an ATM purchase made by Little in Kentucky. He was traced to a Christian Shelter and arrested.

The man denied the murders, and police needed to keep him nearby while they built their case. Back in 2007, he had been arrested in Los Angeles for possession of cocaine. On that occasion he had pleaded guilty, in return for sentencing limited to a drug diversion program. He failed to attend this, and a warrant was issued for his arrest, but it was only applicable in the state of California.

Now Little was back there, answering questions about the three 1980s murders. He was arrested on the outstanding drugs offences, and sentenced to three years imprisonment.

But January of the following year, police had the evidence they needed for the more serious matters, and in 2014, Little was tried and given three terms of life imprisonment for the Los Angeles killings. That was only the beginning.

In fact, this was not the first time that he had been investigated for murder. In 1976, Little was convicted of the ravish rape of Pamela Kay Smith in Sunset Hills, Missouri. Law enforcement realised that they had an even more dangerous criminal on their hands than they previously thought. It seemed as though Little had developed a sexual fascination for strangulation. A perversion that was leading him into ever more serious attacks.

In 1982 a naked, bruised body was found in a field running next to US 27 in Alachua County, Florida. Patricia Ann Mount had been beaten, raped and strangled. Although she was married, the last sight of her had been her dancing with a man, later identified as Little.

Then, later in the year, Melinda LaPree's body was found in a South Mississippi cemetery in the city of Gautier. By the time she was discovered, her body was little more than a skeleton. LaPree had last been seen a month before in Pascagoula. There, witnesses had observed her getting into a brown station wagon, with identifiable wooden panelling.

The driver was thought to be Little, who owned a car like that at the time.

When later in the year, Little was caught shoplifting in Pascagoula, the police department realised that he matched the description of their chief suspect in the case of Melinda LaPree. They charged him with murder, but the grand jury would not indict him.

Next, the authorities switched their attention to the murder of Patricia Mount, in which the involvement of Little was indicated. This time, they managed to get him to trial, but he was acquitted after the jury deliberated for less than half an hour.

'It was a weak case,' admitted the then prosecutor, Ken Hebert. Little's defense attorney, John Kearns, went further.

'There is more doubt that there is fact,' he argued in his closing statement.

Little was freed, but not deterred from his criminal lifestyle. In fact, it is more than possible that he felt himself even more invincible. As soon as October in the same year, police discover Little in the company of a woman. She immediately accuses him of attacking her and Little is arrested. Another assault comes to light and once more Little faces trail for serious offences, this time two accusations of attempted murder. Once more, he escapes full punishment, as the jury cannot decide on a clear verdict. However, this time, Little pleads guilty to false imprisonment and assault, and is sentenced to four years incarceration for the offences. He serves just two and half years and, on release, moves to Los Angeles.

Within six months, Carol Alford is dead. A death which, as we can see, was most probably avoidable.

In the summer of 2018, while serving his triple life sentence, Little was moved to Wise County, Texas, and in October transferred on to Ector County in the same state. During this time, he began to form a relationship with a Texas Ranger, James Holland. Revelations began to emerge as Little developed trust in the Ranger. Then, he confessed to another murder.

Denise Christie Brothers was missing for more than a month when her body was found in a field. She was half naked, had been raped and strangled. Denise had last been seen in a motel parking lot in Odessa in January 1994.

With the admission of this crime, it seemed as though the floodgates opened for Little. He admitted murder after murder to James Holland. Soon, investigators from around the US were visiting Texas to speak to the loose mouthed killer, who had by now been indicted for the murder of Denise. They came not only from Texas but from Florida, Kentucky, Tennessee, Mississippi, Georgia. Little's creeping tendrils reached out to New Mexico and Louisiana, to Illinois and South Carolina. Soon, the FBI and the Justice Department were also involved. 'Little has provided details of more than 90 murders committed in multiple states,' said the Wise County sheriff's office.

'We expect more,' said Bobby Bland, the Ector County District Attorney.

Samuel Little was making headlines.

But, fear some, that notoriety might have been just what he wanted. Little was a prolific but, in terms of convictions, small time crook at least until the multiple murders for which he was convicted in 2014. He is now seventy eight years old; a life of drug and alcohol misuse, of living on the streets, in hostels and out of the back of a car must have taken their toll. He is an intelligent man, he will realise that his life expectancy is poor, and the quality of whatever time he has left will be low. He will never be released from prison – his 2014 conviction was made without the possibility of parole. He has no family, no one to care for or to care for him. To be fair, that had been the case (grandmother apart) for almost the entirety of his life.

Maybe, suspect some, the thought of going down in history as the nation's most prolific serial killer is something that appeals to a man with nothing to lose. A chance of attention and fame. It is almost impossible to feel any sympathy someone such as Little, considering the harm and distress he has caused, even without the murders to which he is now confessing. But knowing that the game is up, that there is nothing ahead except for life in a damp, dangerous, vile smelling place full of hate and bitterness must be hard to take, even when warranted. Might that be enough for him to design his elaborate web of intrigue, and weave it over investigators from across the country?

People confess to crimes they have not committed for many reasons. The investigative journalist and Pulitzer Prize winner Maurice Possley has in depth knowledge of these. 'People confess to crimes they don't commit because they fear the death penalty,' he said, 'because they are mentally ill or they are intellectually handicapped.'

Speaking to CBS News he went on to say, 'They confess because police are smarter and forceful and believe in extracting the truth, even if the facts belie the confession.'

Certainly, there will be many who believe that a man who kills ninety or more women must suffer from some form of mental illness, but beyond this those most common of reasons for admitting to crimes not committed fail to apply in Little's case.

Nor is he young, nor, it would seem, is he intimidated by the police – further reasons identified by Possley as causes of false admissions. Indeed, the confessions Little has made came from his development of a trusting relationship with a Texas Ranger. They are completely voluntary.

But there are many other possibilities behind the confessions. Firstly, in all likelihood, they are the truth. Little had been a key suspect in several murders, it's just that he got away with his crimes for many years. Many of the assaults which resulted in the deaths of those he claims to have killed were not properly investigated. At least, not investigated with the same determination and resilience as would be the case where the victim from a different background. That inevitably means evidence will have been missed.

Thousands of people go missing every year, many end up as the victims of murder. For example, in 2013, 1615 women were killed by men, violently, across the country. There will have been countless others whose identification has not been confirmed, whose disappearance has not been solved. Somebody commits these crimes, and many psychologists fear the problem of serial killers is much more widespread than the news media suggests. It is thought that there were at least six of these sociopaths operating in Los Angeles alone in the 1980s. A woman raped and killed by an intruder in their own home makes a disturbing but interesting story; a prostitute going missing, or being discovered in an alley, sells fewer newspapers.

Therefore the probability is that Little's confessions are based in truth. While is it certainly true that from his time in prison he may have heard stories about killings which he is now weaving into his own stories, detectives have identified details that are not generally known in many of the cases. Further, more than a third have already been positively checked out, and it seems highly likely that his confessions are true. Bobby Bland told the press that 'He (Little) has confessed to over 90 murders and they have been able to match over 30 (of these confessions) and continue to make other matches as they go along.' Doubts do still exist over Little's motivations for claiming responsibility for the crimes, but now the likes of legal analyst Nick Leonardo, who says his confessions must be taken 'with a pinch of salt' and that they 'lack veracity', are falling into a minority.

Little is a man, it seems, who has killed approaching a hundred women; that is what he has admitted so far – the final figure could be much higher.

So why is he speaking out now? There are many possibilities. Most likely is a feeling of wanting to unload the guilt he is carrying. Little does not appear to be a particularly religious person, but as the end of life approaches, every doubter wonders a little – perhaps he feels that the weight of his crimes will be lessened come his final judgement day if he has admitted to what he has done.

Possibly he is enjoying the attention he is receiving. However, just because that could be the case does not mean that what he is saying is untrue.

Wise County Sheriff Lane Akin has mixed feelings about the confessions. 'I think it is a tragic situation,' he said, 'but on the other hand there are a lot of people who have been looking for answers probably for more than 30 years and I hope maybe some answers will be provided.'

It is a point echoed by Bobby Bland. 'The rangers and the FBI are constantly trying to confirm these cases throughout this country so we can bring closure to all these families,' he said.

Little is big news at the moment. Becoming, potentially, the USA's most prolific ever serial killer attracts the macabre in all of us. The web is littered with stories and speculation. But despite this, something very important is becoming lost. Details of those women he killed are hard to find. Yes, we can locate their names, the dates of their disappearance and discovery. Sometimes, information is available of the crimes committed against them, often that they were strangled and raped.

But finding out about the lives of these victims is difficult. That problem bookends them as 'victims', rather than real people. Perhaps they are considered not as newsworthy. Perhaps, because in many cases the victims were drug users and prostitutes, their deaths were not considered at the same level of significance as, say, that of a middle class professional mother.

That does not stop them from being real people; they had families – sometimes children, husbands, parents, brothers and sisters. For those relatives, their lives have been changed forever.

Here is one such story. A person behind a victim. Rosie Hill was just twenty years old when her body was found on a roadside in Florida. This was in 1982, and Rosie's mother Minnie still bears the scars of that time. A few days before her August 16th murder, Rosie had phoned her mother to say that she had got herself into some bother, and needed to come home to get away from it. She told her mother that she loved her, and received confirmation of her mother's love in return. Both looked forward to her return home in a couple of days. She would not be heard from again.

Rosie was a young mother herself, who had only lived in Florida for three years. She had grown up in Memphis, where she attended the Booker T Washington High School. For two long years Minnie awaited her daughter's return, but she never arrived. The reason for this eventually became apparent. She had been killed. Rosie's body had, according to her mother, 'deteriorated quick,' but when she had given birth two years before, she had encountered difficulties, and the scars to her internal organs were used to identify her body.

More than thirty years then passed; 'It really tears the family up,' said Minnie. 'I raised her child.'

Detectives had little to go on. Rosie had left a bar with a stranger. Even then, police believed that this man could be Samuel Little, but he had denied any involvement. However, following his recent confession, detectives from Marion County headed to Texas for a two hour interview. 'We talked about Rosie Hill in depth,' said an officer. 'For a 78 year old he was very sharp with details.'

'The lord told me to do it,' claimed Little, referring to the murder of Rosie, which he committed in the back seat of his car before throwing the young woman onto the roadside. Minnie has little idea who this 'Lord' might be. 'A demon, I would say,' she told reporters. 'I would tell him that I forgive him,' said Minnie, when asked what she would say were she to meet her daughter's killer, 'and the rest is between him and the Good Lord. May the Lord have mercy on his soul.'

This forgiveness provides a sharp contrast between good and evil, but nevertheless Minnie continues to suffer daily. 'It's taken thirty six years to get the bad out,' she said. Even now, she knows that the pain will not subside. Neither for her, nor her granddaughter, now a grown woman, who holds only the haziest memories of her mother, if any at all.

Whether or not Samuel Little is found to be responsible for the ninety plus murders to which he has confessed, only time will tell. What we do know is that he killed some women. He focussed on the vulnerable and the troubled. On drug addicts and prostitutes. Not all of his victims belonged to these groups, but, it seems, all were taken in by the apparently intelligent and calming person with whom they met. Then, he changed into a violent, pitiless killer. Certainly, the ingredients of his life contributed significantly to the man he became. But the biggest addition to the pot was his own disregard for the lives of others.

A mixture of different items can produce a meal that is wonderful, satisfying, delicious. But sometimes, sadly, it creates pure poison.

The Footpath Murderer

Natalie Avalon

Colin Pitchfork (Footpath Murderer, Black Pad Killer)

Colin Pitchfork, also known as the Footpath Murderer and the Black Pad Killer was born 23 March 1961 in

Bristol, England. Because Pitchfork's two murders occurred in Leicestershire, the two murders have sometimes been referred to as the Enderby Murders or the Narborough Murders.

The early 20-something Pitchfork—a local baker by trade who was married and had two small sons—was tried, convicted, and sentenced to life for the rape and murder of two 15-year-old girls, Lynda Mann and Dawn Ashworth. He was also convicted for other, earlier, indecent assaults and attempting to pervert the course of justice by enlisting a friend to provide a DNA sample in his place. In fact, Colin Pitchfork has the dubious distinction of being the first person in the world to be convicted with DNA evidence—a new technology at the time. This case is also notable for being the first time where a suspect was cleared based upon DNA testing.

Early Life

Colin Pitchfork was born in Bristol, England, on 23 March 1961, the second of three children, to a housewife mother and miner father. His parents were married and raised all three of their children; however, Pitchfork was oftentimes neglected for affection by his parents who favored his older sister and younger brother over him.

Pitchfork was raised in Newbold Verdon and attended school in Market Bosworth and Desford. While in school Pitchfork was teased because he had matured considerably quicker than his classmates.

In 1979, at the age of 18 he was arrested and convicted of indecent assault after pulling a 16-year-old girl off of a country lane. Instead of indecent assault, his actions could have been more accurately classified as attempted rape. Pitchfork was subsequently referred for therapy at Carlton Hayes Hospital, Narborough, on the Black Pad footpath. The hospital was subsequently closed in 1996; however, the path remains. He had never served time in jail or prison until he was arrested for murder.

In October 1985, Pitchfork dragged another 16-year-old girl into a garage and "indecently assaulted" her while threatening to kill her with a screwdriver. After he was arrested for the two murders, he pled guilty to and was convicted of the assault; however, that he forced his victim to perform oral sex on him is now correctly defined as rape.

On yet another occasion he picked up a blonde hitchhiker named Liz who ended up grabbing the steering wheel in an effort to escape, thus forcing him to release her before he got the chance to rape her.

In 1981 when he was 20 years old, Pitchfork married Carole, a social worker, and the couple moved to

Littlethorpe. Also that year Pitchfork obtained psychiatric counseling at the Woodlands for his sexual proclivities.

The Pitchforks eventually had two sons. The first was born in 1983 and the second in 1986; interestingly the same years Pitchfork committed his two murders.

Carole confessed that while she was pregnant, her husband had become "unsettled" and had resorted to complaining about everything. He was a "the grass is always greener" type who never valued what he had. He would oftentimes say that he wanted a different job, or a bigger house, or something other than what he had. In fact, this extended to his sex life. Despite being married and his wife expecting a baby—twice—Pitchfork often cheated on her. During Carole's first pregnancy, it was a woman named Leslie. Pitchfork had the audacity to bring her over to meet his family, introducing her as a "friend from work." With her second pregnancy it was a woman dubbed "Brown Eyes." She was in the midst of a divorce and already had a child. This was in July 1986 right before Pitchfork's second murder. He had been feeling depressed and went to see a doctor for sleeping pills. The reason for his depression was that "Brown Eyes" was pregnant with his child. He did, however, always want a daughter as his two sons with Carole were obviously not enough so, while depressed, he was also looking forward to having a daughter.

One of Pitchfork's early jobs was as a volunteer at Dr. Barnardo's Children's Home before obtaining long-term work in Hampshire's Bakery in 1976 as an apprentice. He continued to work at the bakery until he was arrested for the murders. His forte was as a cake decorator, particularly sculpting decorations and he had aspirations to start his own cake decorating business someday. His supervisor touted Pitchfork as a "good worker and time-keeper" but "was moody…and he couldn't leave women employees alone." He earned a reputation for talking to and directing considerable attention toward female coworkers, which was oftentimes unwelcomed.

The Crimes

Lynda Mann, 15

15-year-old Lynda Mann was a quiet schoolgirl who enjoyed school and showed a talent for art. On a frigid night, 21 November 1983, Mann went to visit her friend Karen. After leaving Karen's house at approximately 7:30 p.m. she was never seen again. After Mann failed to return home, her justifiably worried parents called the police.

Pitchfork was driving his infant son home when he saw Mann walking along Forest Road near the Black Pad footpath. When she entered the footpath, he parked his car, caught up with her, and exposed himself. Scared, she attempted to run from him but Pitchfork caught up with her and raped her on some land adjacent to the footpath before strangling her to death with her own scarf.

He murdered Mann to prevent her identifying him. He admitted to police that before he raped her, she had said, "What about your wife?" which indicated that she had seen his wedding ring and knew he was married. He also knew that he was wearing an earring and had realized he was losing his hair; both of which could help Mann identify him. He also told investigators that, at the time, he was planning on moving to Littlethorpe, near Narborough—Mann's hometown—and that there was a great likelihood that she would see him in the area. Thus, he decided that he ought to murder her and tie up that nasty loose end that could potentially get him arrested.

The next morning, Mann was found raped and strangled on the Black Pad footpath that was situated between a cemetery and Carlton Hayes

Psychiatric. Her clothes were strewn about and she was strangled with her own scarf.

The forensic evidence—most notably lack of any bruising or other pre-mortem injuries—suggest that Pitchfork first strangled Mann and then raped her as evidenced by the lack of pre-mortem injuries, despite the medical examiner's findings that Mann had been brutally raped.

When 22-year-old Pitchfork attacked Mann, his infant son was asleep in the back seat of his car. He raped and strangled her before driving home and putting his son to bed.

Semen was collected from the body and it was determined that the perpetrator was a secretor which means that his blood type is identifiable in other bodily fluids. It was determined that the murderer had type A blood with a +1 phosphoglucomutase (PGM) enzyme. This profile was applicable to approximately ten percent of adult males in England at the time which led to the police DNA dragnet that will be discussed later.

Dawn Ashworth, 15

On 31 July 1986, 15-year-old Dawn Amanda Ashworth took a shortcut home along a footpath known as Ten Pound Lane on her way home from her job at a newsstand in Enderby. In addition to her parents, she had a younger brother named Andrew.

Ashworth was a student at Lutterworth Grammar School—the same school that Lynda Mann attended. She enjoyed drawing and painting and was very good at them both. Ashworth also liked clothes and music like most teenage girls. Attractive and likeable, Ashworth had many friends, in addition to a reputation as a sensible and mature girl for a 15-year-old.

On that fateful evening, Pitchfork was riding his motorbike and saw Ashworth enter the footpath. He then parked his bike and followed her, caught up with her, and then exposed himself to her. Ashworth tried to run from him but Pitchfork was able to catch her. He raped her in a field adjacent to the footpath.

Not unlike Lynda Mann, Pitchfork murdered Ashworth to prevent her from identifying him. Also like Mann, he strangled Ashworth with her own scarf and then hid her body under some loose foliage.

Two days later on 2 August her body was found a mere mile from where Lynda Mann's body was found three years ago and like Mann, she had been raped and strangled. Ashworth's body was "buried" under heavy brush and hay. However, Ashworth's body contained considerable pre-mortem injuries, thus suggesting that she put up a considerable struggle against her assailant and was raped before she was murdered.

Semen samples taken from Ashworth's body matched the semen taken from Mann's body.

After Pitchfork murdered Ashworth, he returned home and baked a cake.

Ashworth was buried in the cemetery behind St. John the Baptist Church in Enderby in a plot adjacent to where Lynda Mann was buried, thanks to church administrators who offered the Ashworths the plot.

Despite Ashworth's case being reenacted and featured on *Crimewatch*

UK in December 1986, police failed to identify and apprehend the assailant because of the lack of evidence to link Pitchfork—the real murderer—to the victim or the crime.

Investigation

Former 14-year Los Angeles Police Department officer turned best-selling author Joseph Wambaugh wrote a book about the Pitchfork case entitled *The Blooding* (1995) that details the crimes, the advent of DNA testing, and the difficulties faced by the police in investigating the crimes. Many of the quotations in this discussion are from Wambaugh's book.

Police, under the leadership of Chief Superintendent David Baker, examined all of the similarities of the two cases: both occurred along relatively obstructed-from-view footpaths; the victims were both teenage girls walking alone; they were both raped and strangled; they were from the same area, even attending the same school, as previously mentioned; and their bodies were found in similar conditions and close to one another.

They concluded that the same person murdered both girls before forensics proved this fact.

DNA Profiling

The initial prime suspect in the case was 17-year-old Richard Buckland; a local youth with learning disabilities who worked in the kitchen at the local psychiatric hospital not far from the two footpaths where the girls were found. He was considered to be the prime suspect because he had revealed knowledge of Ashworth's body and the crime scene; information that only the killer would know as it wasn't anything in the papers that the general public would be aware of. He also could not account for his whereabouts during the time when Ashworth was killed. After a lengthy and grueling 15-hour interrogation, Buckland finally confessed to Ashworth's murder but repeatedly denied having anything to do with Mann's murder three years earlier. In all actuality, he would have only been 14 at the time anyway. Nevertheless, despite all of Buckland's protestations, police believed that he killed both girls.

The DNA samples were taken to geneticist Dr. Alec Jeffreys at the University of Leicester. Along with Peter Gill and Dave Werrett of the Forensic Science Service (FSS), the three men developed the earliest form of DNA testing and detailed the technique in a 1985 paper. In it, Gill stated that he was responsible for developing the DNA extraction techniques and demonstrating that it was, in fact, possible to obtain DNA profiles from old stains. Of particular interest and usefulness in the Pitchfork case was the capability of developing "the preferential extraction method that was able to differentiate sperm cells from vaginal cells to facilitate the use of DNA evidence in cases of sexual assault."

Dr. Jeffreys said that he accidentally discovered DNA fingerprinting—what he called it—while researching hereditary diseases and concluded that—like fingerprints—an individual's DNA was completely unique; except for identical twins who shared the same DNA as they shared the same fingerprints. He used the restriction fragment length polymorphism (RFLP) technique which seeks to identify and exploit the variations in homologous (or similar) DNA sequences. In this type of analysis, a DNA sample is divided into pieces which have restriction enzymes added to them and the resulting fragments are then separated by gel electrophoresis according to their lengths. The procedure, at the time, was relatively inexpensive and enjoyed widespread application, such as in the Pitchfork case where officers obtained genetic samples from every male in the area where the murders occurred whose blood matched the killer's blood type that was identified because he was a secretor and his blood type was available through the semen he left inside of his victims. Historically, RFLP analysis was a critical tool in genome mapping, in localizing genes to identify genetic disorders and to determine risk for disease, and in paternity testing. The Pitchfork case was the first time DNA testing was used in a criminal case.

Using the preferential extraction method, Dr. Jeffreys compared semen samples collected from both Mann's and Ashworth's bodies and further analysis demonstrated that both girls were, indeed, killed by the same man. The testing also proved that Buckland was not the murderer and he was subsequently cleared and released.

Of course, the police were mildly irritated because they believed that the murderer was in custody and they had little faith in this new science. After contacting the FSS and having another analysis done, the results corroborated Dr. Jeffreys' findings. Thus, Buckland became the first person in history to have his innocence proven through DNA fingerprinting. Dr. Jeffreys added that he had "no doubt whatsoever" that Buckland would have been found guilty without the definitiveness of DNA testing.

Buckland was released after serving four months in jail.

The question remains as to why had Buckland confessed. Some speculate that he likely found the body which is how he knew some information that was not made available in the news. This, coupled with the relentless pressure of an exceedingly long and grueling interrogation made him yield under pressure.

The Blooding

Now that Buckland had been cleared, the search for the real murderer began. The FSS and Leicestershire Constabulary initiated a DNA dragnet in which 5,000 local men were asked to volunteer blood and saliva samples with the hopes of finding the real murderer. This process is referred to as "blooding" and was from where Wambaugh got his book's title. This investigation manhunt targeted all local men between the ages of 16 and 34. After six months, the police were no closer to identifying and apprehending the offender than they had been at the outset.

Pitchfork wholeheartedly believed in the science of DNA testing and used his cunning and conniving mind to formulate a way out of the testing. He enlisted the assistance of a friend, Ian Kelly, who was not required to test as he did not live in the targeted area, and got him to donate his DNA in Pitchfork's place.

The two men got passport photos of Kelly and Pitchfork expertly swapped the photo in his own passport. He had done such a good job that the police did not suspect a thing; something for which they would be criticized later.

After Kelly gave the sample for Pitchfork, the latter had to "make it look good"; that he, in fact, was tested. Pitchfork, therefore, scratched a mark on his inner forearm with a compass needle and then applied an adhesive plaster. When he got home that afternoon, Carole commented that she thought it would only be a pinprick but Pitchfork, ever the exaggerator, made a huge brouhaha about, first, removing the plaster which he did as though he were removing sutures, and second, how much his arm hurt.

When the letter came that told Pitchfork that he was not, in fact, the murderer, Carole was extremely relieved. But her relief would prove to be short-lasting.

Arrest

Pitchfork may have not been apprehended for some time save for a stroke of luck. On 1 August 1987, while drinking at a Leicester pub, Pitchfork's friend and coworker, Ian Kelly, confessed to others that Pitchfork had given him £200 for giving a DNA sample while pretending to be Pitchfork. Allegedly, Pitchfork had told Kelly that he had already given his sample under another friend's name because that friend had a prior conviction for burglary when he was a youth and wanted to avoid any police harassment. Since Kelly was not a local man, he was not part of the investigation and, therefore, not required to volunteer a biological sample. Had it not been for a woman sitting nearby who had overheard the conversation and reported it to the police, Pitchfork would not have been identified and arrested, and more women would have likely been raped and murdered.

Pitchfork was arrested at his home on Haybarn Close in Littlethorpe on 19 September 1987. The officers waited for his blue Fiat to enter the cul-de-sac and for the family to enter the house safely. Then Derek Pearce and Gwynne Chambers went around the house to cover the back door. The "two Micks"—Mick Thomas and Mick Mason—went to the front door and Phil Beeken and Brian Fentum backed up the two Micks. At 5:45 p.m. Thomas knocked on the door. Carole answered, initially believing them to be insurance agents. When they entered the house the two Micks identified themselves as police officers who needed to speak to her husband privately.

Mason asked Pitchfork, "Why Dawn Ashworth?" Pitchfork replied, "Opportunity. She was there and I was there." When Pitchfork spoke to his wife, she asked him if he did, in fact, murder the two girls. He admitted that yes, he was. She flew at her husband, beyond angry, and had to be stopped by Thomas before inflicting any serious harm upon her husband. She did manage to punch Pearce in the mouth and kick him in the groin.

In the police car Pitchfork told the officers, "I *must* let a few people know what's happened to me before they read it in the papers," and then, he said, he would tell them everything. He added, "[I]t's really a story of my life, not just the story of a month of two."

A DNA sample taken was found to match the murderer. He was the 4,583rd man tested in the England DNA "blooding" dragnet.

Pitchfork admitted that he had flashed females in excess of 1,000 times during his life and that this behavior was a compulsion started when he was in his early teens. He stated that flashing led to sexual assault which led to strangling in order to protect his identity.

With respect to the Ashforth murder, investigators had asked myriad questions and the entire time Pitchfork was being questioned he acted like he was being put out and that investigators were insulting his intelligence. He had said that he initially thought he ought to rob his victim because he saw ten pounds in her purse but then thought better of it because he wasn't sure how he would explain ten quid to Carole.

Police confronted him about the brutality of his rape of Ashworth as she was "torn up pretty badly." They asked if he knew that she was a virgin and Pitchfork said that she told him halfway through the rape. They also asked him about injuries to her bottom and asked him if he knew what he had done. Pitchfork had said that he wasn't in complete control over what he was doing but that he "can *relive* it second by second." Again, obviously annoyed like any reasonably-adept sociopath when confronted with other people's consciences which he views as a weakness, Pitchfork admitted that he knew that he was "talking about it coldheartedly."

He also added that Ashworth "died a damn sight quicker than Lynda Mann" because, with Mann, he didn't go straight for her carotid artery to cut off the blood flow to her brain. Pitchfork added that doing so was a recognized Japanese way of killing and that he'd been trained in judo and would any of the interrogators like for him to demonstrate the technique on one of them. They were not impressed with his stories.

Pitchfork also told investigators that he lost his watch at the scene and inquired as to whether anyone found it.

Throughout the interrogation investigators noticed that Pitchfork would leave out pertinent details about his activities that would make him appear unmanly or something like that. For example, when asked about his flashing over 1,000 girls in his youth he vehemently denied that he masturbated in front of them and any mention of premature ejaculation was immediately shut down. Pitchfork also blamed Mann and Ashworth for walking through open gates on their own, just inviting trouble, while he tried to let them pass. He would also never admit that he sodomized Ashworth.

Trial and Sentence

The day after his arrest, Pitchfork was taken to his first remanding at Castle Court, an old English court that looked like one would imagine it to; complete with stone walls and oak pillars, arched windows, and some blackened ceiling beams that dated back to 1105 A.D. Brian Escott-Cox was the prosecuting barrister, David Farrer was Pitchfork's defense counsel, and Mr.

Justice Philip Otton oversaw the proceedings.

Pitchfork was charged with and confessed to two murders, as well as two additional separate indecent assaults from 1979 and 1985, and he also admitted attempting to pervert the course of justice by enlisting Kelly to provide his own DNA sample on Pitchfork's behalf. Pitchfork pled not guilty to the kidnapping of Liz, the hitchhiker, who he had "spared" for some reason that even Pitchfork could not accurately iterate.

Farrer said during the hearing

that Pitchfork would be "forever haunted by the images and knowledge of what he has done"; however, the court psychiatrist stated that the hauntings of a psychosexual sociopath does not constitute horror but "inspiration." The psychiatrist classified Pitchfork as an opportunistic, non-compulsive, sexual sociopath who only decides to offend when he sees a potential victim. This differs from those sexual serial killers who stalk their victims or who have a specific "type" for whom they look.

Justice Otton, upon Pitchfork's sentencing, stated that the rapes were particularly sadistic and had it not been for the advent of DNA testing, there was a great likelihood that Pitchfork could still be free and many other women would be in danger. Otton sentenced Pitchfork to two life sentences for the murders, ten years for the two "indecent assaults" in 1979 and 1985, and three years for "perverting the course of justice" by evading the DNA testing and getting Ian Kelly to submit his DNA in his place." Per the Home Secretary, Michael Howard,

Pitchfork's minimum term, or tariff, was set at 30 years, which meant that Pitchfork would have to serve at least 30 years before becoming eligible for parole. After an appeal, Pitchfork's sentence was reduced by two years.

Ian Kelly was given an 18-month suspended sentence for his part in conspiring with Pitchfork to hide his DNA.

After the sentencing, the media wanted to interview Dawn Ashworth's family but they denied the request. Instead, an older interview with the family during the investigation was aired in February 1988. In this old footage, Ashworth's mother Barbara stated—when asked about potentially forgiving her daughter's murderer—that she has to forgive or she would feel "very bitter and twisted" and that's not a way to live. Her father Robin said, "I don't feel any hate or wish for any revenge for the murder of Dawn, because it's not going to do any good." However, once Pitchfork was sentenced and the DNA evidence proved conclusively that Pitchfork was, in fact, the murderer, Robin said that he wanted the death penalty reintroduced. Further, in a public poll, 96% of the public was in agreement for bringing back the hangman in cases such as this.

Lynda Mann's mother and stepfather, Kath and Eddie Eastwood, as well as her sister Rebecca Eastwood, have been vocal about how Pitchfork should never be paroled. In fact, Rebecca created an online petition specifically to halt any potential parole hearing should one actually arise seeing as how Pitchfork is scheduled for a parole hearing sometime in 2016. As of

January 2016, Rebecca has collected 17,000 signatures, much to her own surprise and delight.

Baker was also interviewed following Pitchfork's sentencing as the police were under considerable scrutiny for their failure to identify and apprehend Pitchfork earlier. Baker was asked why Pitchfork was never questioned given his flashing background. He was also criticized for his people allowing an altered passport to get by them—this passport being the one that Pitchfork "adjusted" with Ian Kelly's photograph. Other questions included why Pitchfork wasn't fingerprinted and photographed in all of his previous brushes with the law. Baker had said that one reason was that, at the time, flashing was considered only a nuisance and not a "real" crime. Baker also added that the victims of Pitchfork's earlier assaults would likely not have been able to pick his mugshot out of a photo parade because the assaults occurred late at night and Pitchfork altered his appearance by growing or shaving facial hair.

Appeal

On 14 May 2009, Pitchfork's appeal was heard at the Royal Courts of Justice in London. He was granted a two-year reduction to his original 30-year sentence. Consequently, Pitchfork was eligible to apply for parole in September 2015 due to the time served spent upon remand prior to his conviction and this was postponed until early 2016. However, the Lord Chief Justice stated that Pitchfork could not be released "unless and until the safety of the public is assured."

Since he has been incarcerated, the 52-year-old Pitchfork has educated himself to degree level and had achieved proficiency in the transcription of printed music into Braille with the hope, one day, of being able to help the blind. His defense team presented this evidence as indication of the development of Pitchfork's character while incarcerated.

Aftermath

Artwork and Sales Proceeds Controversy

In April 2009, a sculpture that

Pitchfork had created in prison was exhibited at the Royal Festival Hall on London's South Bank. The artwork—called "Bringing Music to Life"—depicted an orchestra and choir made "in meticulous miniature detail by folding, cutting and tearing the score of Beethoven's Ninth Symphony." The sculpture was purchased by the Royal Festival Hall for £600 and was subsequently exhibited as part of a venture by the Koestler Trust that was originally founded by novelist Arthur Koestler and runs an awards contest for inmates. Initially presented anonymously, when the sculptor's identity was finally revealed in April 2009, the revelation was met with both astonishment and anger from crime victims' groups. Compounding the problem was that Pitchfork profited financially from the sale of his sculpture; earning £300 of the sale proceeds himself. Per the Trust's policy, the artist receives half of the sale proceeds, the charity retains 40% themselves, and 10% goes to victim support.

However, outrage in the *Daily Mail* due to Pitchfork's past and why he had been incarcerated led to the sculpture's removal; particularly since he had fashioned it while incarcerated at Frankland Prison, Brasside, Durham. Pitchfork's caption for the sculpture was, "Without this opportunity to show our art, many of us would have no incentive, we would stay locked in ourselves as much as the walls that hold us."

Lynda Mann's mother Kath said that "paying her daughter's 'evil, wicked and cruel' killer of his work showed a 'lack of conscience.'" She added that he is in prison as punishment for his horrendous crime and for violating Rawls' social contract theory and that should never be forgotten. Additionally, Kelvin Donaghey—a family friend of Dawn Ashworth—created a memorial website to both Ashworth and Mann. He stated that both girls were very good at art and they never got the chance to see their own work exhibited; however, the man who brutally murdered them gets to display his own plus earn compensation from it and that was wrong. In response, Tim Robertson, chief executive of the Koestler Trust stated that the person's offense is irrelevant as the quality of the art is more important. He added that the charity makes no distinction between artists' crimes but only releases their names when given written permission by both the inmate artist and the Prison Service. However, the charity failed to obtain that permission. Eventually, Royal Festival Hall officials removed the artwork from display and apologized for any ill-will harbored and any offense caused and while it respected the Trust's policy, future policy would, indeed, be reviewed.

Those who see no problem with the arrangement state that if an inmate is attempting to rehabilitate himself and improve his life while incarcerated then society "should be pleased by that rather than condemning him or trying to stop him from benefiting from the proceeds." In fact, Pitchfork is not the only criminal to profit from prison-produced art. East End gangster Ronnie Kray painted a series of eight landscapes on prison issue cards while incarcerated during the 1970s which subsequently sold for £16,550 at auction. Additionally, Jimmy Boyle

—"the most violent man in Scotland"—became a prison sculptor and later wrote his own autobiography which was later made into a film entitled *A Sense of Freedom* (1981). Further, Charles Bronson, also known as Charles Arthur "Charlie" Salvador and born as Michael Gordon "Mickey" Peterson—"Britain's most dangerous inmate" and the topic of the 2008 film *Bronson*—has received at least 11 Koestler awards for his poetry and art.

Pitchfork's cunning, however, rests upon the fact that his art unveiling coincided with an upcoming High Court appeal to demonstrate that he could be a productive and upstanding member of society. Ongoing criticism ensues, particularly with the potentially offensive title of his work—"Bringing Music to Life"—as well as the message beside the sculpture Pitchfork penned.

In 2014, a two-part television miniseries entitled *Code of a Killer* was commissioned and broadcast in two 90-minutes episodes on 6 and 13 April 2015. It was based on Pitchfork's crimes and the creation of DNA profiling. The program starred John Simm and Dr. Jeffreys, David Threlfall as Baker, and Nathan Wright as Pitchfork.

Dr. Alec Jeffreys was knighted by the Queen in 1994.

THE KILLER DOCTOR

KATE WELLS

Dr. Harold Frederick Shipman was known in England as "Dr. Death." He is one of the most prolific serial killers in recorded history who, between 1974 and 1998, was suspected of killing over 215 of his patients by poisoning them with lethal injections of morphine. He was ultimately found guilty of 15 murders and sentenced to life in prison, never to be released. Shipman committed suicide while in prison on 13 January 2004.

Early Life

Born on 14 January 1946 in Nottingham, England, Harold Frederick

Shipman, known as "Fred" or "Freddy", was the middle of Vera's and Harold Shipman Sr.'s three children. He had a sister Pauline who was seven years his senior and a brother Clive who was four years younger. His father was a lorry driver and his parents were devout Methodists. Shipman's childhood was far from normal thanks to his mother's influence; who instilled within him an early sense of superiority that served to taint his social relationships turning him into an isolated adolescent with few friends. According to a neighbor at the time, Shipman's mother was friendly but believed and acted as if her family was superior to everyone else. The neighbor also commented that

Shipman was obviously his mother's favorite child; the one in whom she saw the greatest potential.

Vera dominated virtually every aspect of Shipman's life. She decided with whom he could play and when. She dictated what he wore and in order to distinguish him from the other children made him wear a tie even when his siblings were permitted more casual dress. In elementary school, Shipman was rather bright and performed reasonably well but his performance reduced to mediocrity when he reached higher levels. He was, however, determined to succeed and continued plodding along until he achieved his goal. This trait would follow him into adulthood when he had to retake his medical school entrance examinations after failing the first time.

There is much literature that suggests that Shipman had every opportunity to fit in and be part of a group. He was an accomplished football player and track runner; however, his air of superiority was his fundamental obstacle in cultivating meaningful friendships and other relationships with his peers. Throughout school—and even during medical school—his peers and teachers remarked that they barely remembered Shipman and those who did said that he often looked down upon them and seemed amused by the way his peers behaved. He was universally remembered as a loner even though he was far more sociable during medical school than his mother had ever permitted him to be. Such aloofness extended to his romantic relationships where nobody remembered Shipman ever having a girlfriend. In fact, he had taken his sister to school dances.

Shipman was especially close to his mother who died of lung cancer when he was just 17 years old. When she was first diagnosed, Shipman willingly cared for her and was fascinated with the effect morphine had on relieving her suffering. Her death would serve as the model for his subsequent modus operandi. During the last stages of her life, Vera's doctor made regular house calls and she was injected with morphine to ease her pain. Shipman repeatedly witnessed his mother's pain subside as a result of the morphine until she died on 21 June 1963. There is much speculation that his mother's death provided the impetus for his choice of career as a physician and his subsequent murderous spree.

In fact, the literature suggests that Shipman's behavior during the days leading up to her death closely paralleled what his behavior would be like as the most prolific serial killer in English history. Every day after school he would rush home, make his mother a cup of tea and sit and talk to her about his day. She looked very forward to this time; counting the minutes until he was home from school. Many suggest that this is where Shipman learned his endearing bedside manner that would make his patients adore him when he became a physician. When she was in severe pain—self-administration painkiller pumps had not been developed at this time—Vera's sole relief was courtesy of the family doctor. Shipman would watch in fascination as a shot of morphine had the tremendous power to alleviate his mother's distress. This image left an indelible mark on the impressionable 17-year-old who would later recreate it hundreds of time with his own patients.

Following her death Shipman was bound

and determined to go to medical school. He was awarded a scholarship to the Leeds School of Medicine and graduated in 1970. Shortly thereafter he interned at Pontrefract General Infirmary in Pontrefract, West Riding of Yorkshire.

It was during this time he met his wife-to-be Primrose when he was 19. They married when she was 17 and already five months pregnant with their first child. Primrose's upbringing was eerily similar to Shipman's in that her mother restricted her friendships and controlled her behavior. Not a particularly attractive woman, she was, nevertheless, delighted to finally have a boyfriend.

In 1974—now a father of two—Shipman

took a position as a general practitioner at the Abraham Ormerod Medical Centre in Todmorden, West Yorkshire. Interestingly, his hard work and enthusiasm enabled him to fit well into social circles. His senior colleagues—especially Dr. Michael Grieve—viewed him as a godsend who was able to keep them abreast of recent medical developments since he was fresh out of medical school.

Shipman started to suffer blackouts and he told his colleagues that he had epilepsy. His lies surfaced when the office receptionist, Marjorie Walker, found some disturbing entries in one of the druggist's controlled narcotics ledger. The records indicated that

Shipman had been prescribing frequent and excessive amounts of pethidine—a synthetic form of morphine—in several patients' names. In a covert investigation by Dr. John Dacre, senior physician at the practice, proof that many of the patients on the ledger list neither required nor received the medication emerged.

When confronted with the discrepancy and the fact that the medication had found its way "into [Shipman's] very own veins" he first begged for a second chance and, when denied, became enraged, hurled a medical bag to the ground, threatened to resign, and stormed out. His colleagues were astounded at his violent and rather uncharacteristic behavior. Shortly thereafter, Shipman's wife stormed into the room where his peers were discussing how best to dismiss Shipman and, rather rudely, told them that her husband would never resign and that he would have to be forced out. One enduring question remained: did Shipman inject all of the stolen drugs into his own veins or had he already started killing his patients?

Shipman was fined £600 for forgery and attended The Retreat—a private drug rehabilitation clinic in York—for a brief time after being asked to leave his previous job. It is interesting to note that even after being fined for attempted forgery, Shipman's inflated self-image precluded him from realizing that his skill in this area was pathetic and that his ineptitude was easily exposed. This would be important when Shipman later attempted to forge one of his victim's signatures on a will. His unwavering arrogance and lack of judgment would contribute to his downfall.

After serving briefly as a medical officer for Hatfield College in Durham and doing some temporary work for the National Coal Board, Shipman became a general practitioner at the Donneybrook Medical Centre in Hyde, Greater Manchester in 1977. His colleagues trusted him; however, he had a reputation for being arrogant toward junior staff. Whereas today it would be unlikely that given his past Shipman would have been permitted to have access to controlled substances, at the time there were no restrictions and he was back in business. He was readily accepted by his colleagues and members of the community—yet another testament to his complete self-confidence and manipulative and persuasive demeanor.

Shipman did tell colleague Dr. Jeffery Moysey that he had had a problem with pethidine, had undergone treatment, and was now clean. He added that all Dr. Moysey could do was to trust and watch him for unusual or questionable behavior. Obviously, Shipman was not watched nearly closely enough.

Soon, Shipman reassumed his role as a

dedicated, community-minded, hardworking physician and soon gained his patients' unwavering trust and his colleagues' respect; however, his subordinates repeatedly commented on his abusive and sarcastic persona which Shipman adeptly hid in front of those he wanted to impress.

Concerned about the unusually high rate of deaths and the curious similarities surrounding the condition of Shipman's patients at the time of their death—most were fully clothed and either sitting up in a chair or reclining in a settee fully clothed instead of in bed in their night clothes as was normally the case with elderly patients on their death beads—local undertaker Alan Massey questioned Shipman in March 1988 who told him that there was nothing to be concerned about. While Massey accepted Shipman at his word and took no further action, his daughter Debbie Brambroffe, also a funeral director, was not so easily assuaged. She approached Dr. Susan Booth who had also found the pattern disturbing. From a neighboring practice and pursuant to British law that required a doctor from an unrelated practice to countersign cremation forms issued by the original doctor, Dr. Booth was frequently called to Hyde funeral directors. These "witnesses" are then paid a fee for their service which many practitioners referred to as "cash for ash."

Dr. Booth shared her concerns with colleagues. One of them, Dr. Linda Reynolds of the Brook Surgery contacted coroner John Pollard who notified the police. Following a covert investigation that was highly questionable due to its seeming incompleteness, Shipman was cleared on the simple basis that his records seemed to be in order and authorities failed to contact the General Medical Council, or even check criminal records, which would have yielded evidence of his past record.

In 1983 Shipman was interviewed for the documentary *World in Action* about community treatment for the mentally ill and in 1993 Shipman—already a highly respected member of the community—founded his own surgery on Market Street.

The Crimes

Every one of Shipman's victims died from a fatal dose of morphine. A complete alphabetical list of all 215 people he murdered can be found at: http://www.theguardian.com/uk/2002/jul/19/shipman.health2.

The index case was Shipman's final victim before his arrest: former ceremonial Hyde Mayor Kathleen Grundy, an active and wealthy 81-year-old widow who was found dead in her house on 24 June 1998 when she failed to make an appearance at the Age Concern Club where she regularly served meals to elderly pensioners. When her friends and family went to check on her, Grundy was dead. They immediately called Shipman who had paid Grundy a visit mere hours earlier and was the last to see her alive. He claimed that the purpose of his visit was to take blood samples for a study on aging. Shipman pronounced Grundy dead and her daughter, Angela Woodruff, also a solicitor, was notified. Shipman told Woodruff that any postmortem examination was unnecessary seeing as how he had just seen her mother prior to her death.

After Grundy's burial, Woodruff received a troubling phone call from solicitors who claimed to have a copy of her mother's will. Since Woodruff's agency handled her mother's affairs she found this suspicious and examined the document that was so poorly typed that it made no sense and it contained a strange signature at the bottom. After initially thinking that Shipman may have been framed, she soon realized that he had killed her mother for profit and called the police.

Investigation

Investigation into Shipman's activities proved to be a long and arduous endeavor. As mentioned, Massey's daughter expressed concern regarding Shipman's patients that reached Dr. Reynolds who subsequently expressed her concerns to South Manchester District coroner John Pollard. Reynolds was particularly concerned about the large number of cremation forms for Shipman's elderly female patients which required countersignatures. She suspected Shipman of killing his patients but was not sure if this occurred through negligence or intent. The complaint ultimately reached Detective Superintendent Bernard Postles who took over the investigation and immediately determined the will to be a fake and began to look more closely at Shipman.

When police were first notified of the suspicions levied against Shipman, officers were unable to find sufficient evidence to warrant bringing charges against Shipman. After the fact when all of the evidence in the Shipman case was brought to light, police were blamed for assigning inexperienced officers to the case and subsequently abandoning the investigation. Later, *The Shipman Inquiry* uncovered that between the time police abandoned the investigation on 17 April 1998 and the time of Shipman's arrest, he had killed three more people; his last being Grundy. It was ultimately Grundy's daughter Woodruff whose personal investigation into her mother's death provided the impetus to fully scrutinize Shipman and learn the full extent of his murderous ways.

Woodruff became suspicious when solicitor Brian Burgess informed her about a will her mother had allegedly made that excluded Woodruff and her children but left £386,000 to Shipman. As her mother was always meticulous in her affairs, Woodruff seriously doubted that her mother had anything to do with the new will that superseded her previous one and could tell immediately that the signature on the will had been forged. At Burgess' urging, Woodruff reported her concerns about her suspicions into the forged will to the police who renewed their investigation.

Grundy's body had to be exhumed for examination. This was a very rare occurrence for British police as the majority of officers had never experienced one. They requested assistance from the National Crime Squad and Postles and crew would soon become uncomfortably unfamiliar with the process when they had to exhume 11 additional bodies of which eight were used in the criminal indictment. When Grundy's body was exhumed and examined it was found to contain traces of diamorphine. The medical examiner concluded that the deadly dose of morphine was administered within three hours prior to her death—exactly when Shipman had paid her a visit.

Following Shipman's arrest the typewriter on which the forged will was created was found in his house; along with medical records and an odd collection of jewelry. Further investigation into other deaths that Shipman had certified yielded a list of

15 cases that required further review and during this investigation the authorities discovered a pattern of Shipman administering lethal overdoses of diamorphine, signing his patients' death certificates, and then forging medical records to suggest that they had been in poor health which contributed to their deaths.

Further investigation generated additional troubling evidence. Shipman had urged the families of his patients to cremate their loved ones in inordinately large numbers while telling them that no further investigation of their deaths was necessary, even in those cases where the deceased had died of causes which were unknown to the families. If families pressed him for questions, Shipman would provide computer-generated medical notes that corroborated his cause of death determinations. Investigators would later discover that Shipman altered his medical notes shortly after killing his patients to ensure that his records matched the outcome. In Grundy's case Shipman had backdated and fabricated several entries in her medical records to give the impression that she was a morphine junkie.

Subsequent investigations began with those patients who had died following a Shipman house call and were not cremated because procurement of tissue samples for postmortem examination is easier.

Several bodies were exhumed and examined. Next, police focused upon the cremated remains of other victims. Investigation into these victims was based primarily on preexisting known conditions, recorded causes of death, and the fact that Shipman was present shortly before they died.

Additional investigation into Shipman's forged computerized records was another area that provided considerable evidence that would be used against him at trial. When Shipman first encountered the computer he was technophobic but in true Shipman fashion soon declared himself to be an expert. However, he was not aware that the hard drive recorded to the second every phony alteration he made to a patient's records. In a taped interview between Shipman and the Greater Manchester Police when confronted with anomalies in his input of details Shipman claimed he did not recall doing whatever it was of which he was accused. Even when confronted with irrefutable computer evidence that he entered much data that was incorrectly dated and/or placed Shipman failed to acknowledge his actions.

Arrest and Trial

Shipman was arrested on 7 September 1998. His trial commenced on 5 October 1999 and was presided over by Mr. Justice Thayne Forbes. Shipman was charged with the murders of Marie West,

Irene Turner, Lizzie Adams, Jean Lilley, Ivy Lomas, Murial Grimshaw, Marie Quinn, Kathleen Wagstaff, Bianka Pomfret, Norah Nuttall, Pamela Hillier, Maureen Ward, Winifred Mellor, Joan Melia, and Kathleen Grundy—all of whom had died between 1995 and 1998.

At the trial's outset Shipman's attorney, 46-year-old Nicola Davies who was predominantly a medical lawyer, presented three applications. First, she alleged that the trial be postponed because she claimed that Shipman could not receive a fair trial because of the prior "inaccurate, misleading" coverage of his case in the media. Prosecutor Richard Henriques—one of the top barristers in all of Britain—countered that the reports alerted other families to potential irregularities regarding the death of their loved ones and was, therefore, beneficial.

Second, Davies wanted the court to hold three separate trials. She argued that the first should be Grundy's because hers was the only one that had a motive: greed. The second one, she argued, should only involve patients who were buried and exhumed because there was physical evidence of the morphine poising. Third, Davies argued that the last trial should cover those cremated due to the lack of physical evidence. Henriques asserted that the interrelated nature of the cases require that they not be severed to present a more comprehensive picture.

Davies' third application requested that evidence referred to in "volume eight" be disallowed during the trial. Volume eight detailed how Shipman acquired and hoarded morphine from 28 patients—many of whom had already died—in addition to continuing to write prescriptions for deceased patients—and keeping the medication for his own purpose. Further, he had prescribed opiates for a number of living patients who had never required strong painkillers such as morphine. After careful consideration, Justice Forbes denied each application. Proceedings were then adjourned until 11 October 1999 when the jury would be selected.

During the trial relatives of Shipman's victims testified and a clear pattern of Shipman's behavior was uncovered. He was portrayed as someone who demonstrated a lack of compassion, disregard for the wishes of his patients' relatives, and reluctance to even attempt to revive patients. Even more troublesome was that he would pretend to call emergency services in the presence of these relatives and then cancel the call when the patient turned out to be deceased. When telephone records were analyzed, Shipman had never made such calls. Additionally, the evidence demonstrated that Shipman hoarded drugs by falsely prescribing morphine to patients who didn't need it, over-prescribing it to others who did, and that he visited the homes of the recently deceased to pick up unused drug supplies for "disposal."

Victim Grundy's daughter Woodruff was an exceptional witness for the prosecution; giving detailed accounts of the conversations she had with Shipman, iterating how meticulous and detailed her mother was in all aspects of her life, talking about how much more in shape Grundy was at 81 than her children, among other compelling information. Similar accounts by other victims' family members would echo Woodruff's testimony; that their loved ones were healthy and that their deaths were suspicious.

Additional witnesses for the prosecution included computer analyst Detective Sergeant John Ashley regarding Shipman's doctoring of his medical records; calligraphy analyst Michael Allen who attested that Shipman's attempted signature forgery of Grundy was a pathetic attempt and, indeed, fraudulent; and pathologist Dr. John Rutherford who explained how the exhumation and subsequent examination on Shipman's victims was conducted, as well as the fact that the only fingerprints on Grundy's new will were those of Shipman and the two witnesses who signed the document—none belonging to the deceased.

During the second week of Shipman's

trial his former colleagues and staff members testified. District nurse Marion Gilchrist described Shipman's reaction when he realized that he would soon be arrested. He allegedly stated that based upon the evidence authorities had he would be found guilty and that the only thing he did wrong was to not have Grundy cremated. Another of Shipman's patients issued a statement regarding what Shipman allegedly told her about Grundy's new will. He purportedly said that if he could bring her back he would because of all the trouble her death has caused and that he was going to say that he didn't want her money but because of all of his troubles he will get it and use some for philanthropic causes.

Finally, Shipman's former colleague Dr. Grenville testified as to how his actions would have been far different than Shipman's if he were in the same situation. Dr. Grenville said that instead of immediately pronouncing Grundy dead he would have carefully examined her body to ensure that death had, in fact, occurred, in addition to attempting to revive her in accordance with standard medical practice.

Evidence of Shipman's litany of lies continued. One glaring commonality was that when he "found" a patient dead he would pretend to call an ambulance. Such was the case with 77-year-old Lizzie Adams, a vibrant woman who enjoyed dancing with her partner William Catlow.

Catlow had, in fact, stopped by to visit Adams on the day she died. He stated that he found Shipman examining her porcelain and crystal collection in the next room as Adams was dying nearby. Catlow testified that she felt warm and that he could feel her pulse. Shipman told him that was Catlow's own pulse and that she had already expired.

Similarly, in the case of Nora Nuttall, her son Anthony testified how he had left his mother alone at home for only 20 minutes and when he returned he found Shipman leaving their house. Shipman allegedly told Anthony that he just called for an ambulance. When Anthony went to his mother she looked asleep but he could not revive her. Soon after, Shipman barely touched her neck and said that he was sorry but she was gone. When Nuttall's sister went to Shipman's office for details of her sister's death, Shipman fabricated lies of how Nuttall called him to say that she was ill and when he was paged he just happened to be in the area and stopped by. When telephone records proved him wrong, Shipman invented a new lie.

Ultimately, the lie regarding his collecting blood from Grundy for some study took the cake. Shipman initially testified that the blood samples had gone for analysis; however, when the prosecution proved that there was no study on aging Shipman suddenly "remembered" that he had left the samples under some notes and when he discovered them they were no longer useful and, thus, he disposed of them.

The myriad lies coupled with Shipman's haughty and arrogant attitude throughout the trial certainly didn't substantiate the defense's attempt to portray him as an old-fashioned caring and dedicated physician who would go out of his way to help his patients. Compounding the problem was that he kept changing his story during questioning.

Additional testimony revealed Shipman to have an utter lack of compassion with respect to announcing his patients' deaths to loved ones; oftentimes being vague enough to make them guess and then berating them for "not listening" to him carefully enough. He even called the neighbor of one of his victims stupid when she confronted him returning to her neighbor's—Gloria Ellis—house and had asked him if Ellis had suffered a stroke. The witness stated that she believed Shipman to be an insurance man instead of a doctor.

One final example of Shipman's callousness occurred when Detective Sergeant Philip Reade visited Shipman's office to locate the next of kin of one Ivy Lomas who was Shipman's only patient to die in his office. Reade said that Shipman was laughing and said that she was "such a nuisance that he was having part of the seating area permanently reserved for Ivy with a plaque to the effect—seat permanently reserved for Ivy Lomas" and that while she "could have taken her last breath" Shipman was busy seeing other patients and made no effort to resuscitate her. Dr. Grenville told the court that the Lomas situation was a medical emergency to which he would have given his complete attention.

In Shipman's defense, Davies had asked the forensic analyst about the validity of testing postmortem tissue for drugs and whether his finding of morphine was proof of single or multiple doses. The scientist said that he couldn't say; however, American pathologist Dr. Karch Steven took the stand and explained the relatively new technique of analyzing hair samples for evidence of ongoing drug use and that in every single case none of Shipman's victims were long-term morphine users.

Shipman also lied about carrying morphine and this lie came back to bite him. After killing his patients he would collect their morphine supplies—which were often overprescribed—for his own "stash." In one case, Jim King was incorrectly diagnosed as having cancer and Shipman treated him with copious amounts of morphine. When King's condition worsened Shipman went to King's house and told him that he needed to give him an injection. King's wife was wary since King's aunt and father had both died after a Shipman visit and she told Shipman that he could write out a prescription. She said that he became increasingly arrogant and snotty.

When the case was ready to go to the jury it took Justice Forbes two weeks to separate all of the evidence presented and to caution jurors that there were no witnesses who saw Shipman kill anyone and to utilize common sense and not react to the anger, disapproval, disgust, or sympathy they had likely felt during the trial. On 31 January 2000 at 4:43 p.m. following six days of deliberation the jury found Shipman guilty of killing 15 patients via lethally injection of diamorphine, and one count of forging Grundy's will. He was sentenced to 15 consecutive life sentences—plus four years for the forgery—and Justice Forbes recommended that Shipman never be released which was later upheld by Home Secretary David Blunkett. Interestingly, this recommendation occurred just a few months prior to Parliament's stripping British government ministers of their power to set minimum terms for convicted offenders.

Shipman never displayed any emotion when the verdict was read. Neither did his wife.

Shipman became the only British doctor in the country's legal history to be found guilty of murdering his patients. While a number of other instances could have been tried, authorities concluded that it would have been difficult for Shipman to have received a fair trial in light of the substantial publicity surrounding his original trial; not to mention that further trials would have been moot given his sentence. Ultimately, *The Shipman Inquiry* estimated the number of Shipman's victims to be as many as 250.

The General Medical Council stripped Shipman of his medical license on 11 February 2000.

Many of his former patients continue to struggle with the possibility that they could have been next and say they owe their lives to Angela Woodruff whose determination to get to the bottom of her mother's suspicious death proved to be Shipman's ultimate demise.

Death

Shipman consistently denied his guilt by disputing the plethora of scientific evidence against him but failed to offer any statements regarding his actions. His wife was also in denial. A number of scientific inquiries were launched in attempts to determine the true extent of Shipman's murderous ways. During these investigations Shipman was incarcerated first in Durham Prison and was transferred to Wakefield Prison in June 2003 to be closer to his family.

Shipman committed suicide at 6:20 p.m. on 13 January 2004, the eve of his 58th birthday, and was pronounced dead at 8:10 p.m. Shipman had hanged himself with bed sheets from the window bars of his cell. Whereas British tabloids expressed joy at his death—as evidenced by a celebratory front-page headline in *The Sun* that said, "Ship Ship hooray," his victims' families stated that they had felt cheated that they would never have the satisfaction of knowing why Shipman did what he did or to hear a confession. Others dubbed him a "cold coward" and condemned the Prison Service for allowing his suicide to occur. Other publications pushed for investigation into the state of Britain's prisons and the welfare of their inmates with some wanting sentencing reform.

Shipman's motive for his suicide was never established although he had reportedly told his probation officer that doing so would ensure that his widow could receive a National Health Service pension and lump sum. In fact, she did receive a full National Health Service pension which would not have occurred had Shipman died after age 60. Further, there continues to be speculation as to when Shipman began killing his patients as well as the exact number of people who died by his hand.

Aftermath

A number of audits and inquiries into Shipman's patients occurred. A clinical audit conducted by University of Leicester Professor Richard Baker examined the number and pattern of deaths of Shipman's patients and compared this figure with similar records from other health care practitioners. Baker found that the rate of death among Shipman's elderly patients was considerably higher, were clustered at certain times of the day, and that Shipman was present in an inordinately high number of cases. Baker's audit estimated that Shipman was likely responsible for at least 236 patient deaths over 24 years.

In January 2001 senior West Yorkshire

detective Chris Gregg was directed to lead an investigation into 22 deaths in his jurisdiction in which Shipman was involved. When the results were submitted in July 2002 it was purported that Shipman had killed at least 215 of his patients between 1975 and 1998 in Todmorden, West Yorkshire, and Hyde.

In a separate inquiry commission chaired by High Court Judge Dame Janet Smith, 500 of Shipman's patients' records were examined and a 2,000-page report concluded that it was highly likely that Shipman murdered at least 218 of his patients with a number of additional suspicious deaths which could not be positively attributed to Shipman. One of them, 67-year-old Margaret

Thompson died in March 1971, shortly after Shipman obtained his medical license, while recovering from a stroke and she is widely believed to be Shipman's first victim. Other potential victims during his early years practicing medicine have never been officially proven.

The majority of Shipman's victims were elderly women who adored their doctor, lived alone and, consequently, were vulnerable. They were in good health before they died. On 24 January 2005, in her sixth report, Smith stated that she believed that Shipman had likely killed seven more patients including a four-year-old girl when Shipman was in the early stages of his career at Pontrefract General Hospital. She increased her estimation to 250; however, because 459 people died while under his care the exact number of victims is unknown.

Shipman's motive for killing is also unknown. As is the case with most serial killers there is usually some motive, some toying with victims to reinforce their power over them, or some smoking gun but all of Shipman's victims died peacefully and all but one did so in the comfort of their own homes. Some speculation asserts that he hated older women and thought that the elderly were a drain on the health care system while others believed he was simply recreating his own mother's death to satisfy some sort of need. The majority, however, believe that Shipman's own self-perceived superiority made him believe that he could do whatever he wanted without fear of apprehension despite that he had been caught for forging prescriptions years ago.

At Smith's urging in *The Shipman Report*, the General Medical Council charged six additional physicians who signed cremation forms for some of Shipman's victims with misconduct, alleging that they should have noticed a pattern between Shipman's house calls and his patients' deaths. These physicians were acquitted.

A 2005 inquiry into Shipman's suicide alleged that it could not have been predicted or prevented but that the prison procedures should be reexamined.

Also in 2005 Shipman was suspected of having stolen some of his victims' jewelry as over £10,000 worth had been found in his garage in 1998. Despite Shipman's widow urging for it to be returned to her the police notified Shipman's victims' families asking them whether they could identify it.

On 30 July 2005 in Hyde Park, the Garden of Tranquility was opened as a memorial garden to Shipman's victims. As of 2009 many of his victims' families are seeking compensation for the loss of their loved ones.

GRANNY KILLER

NATALIE MARSHALL

John Wayne Glover ("The Granny Killer")

John Wayne Glover—also known as the "Granny Killer"—was a serial killer who was active in Sydney, Australia, between 1989 and 1990 who murdered at least six—and as many as 13—elderly females after hitting them with a claw hammer and then ritually strangling them with their own pantyhose. It was widely believed that Glover's victims represented his mother and mother-in-law who he blamed for his misdeeds. He was ultimately sentenced to six life sentences without any possibility of release. Glover committed suicide by hanging himself on 9 September 2005.

Glover's importance in Australian history was that he was the first modern serial killer in Sydney and despite police ultimately catching him, one woman would lose her life as police waited outside of her door while surveilling their prime suspect.

Early Life

John Wayne Glover was born on 26 November 1932 in Wolverhampton, England. He was convicted of numerous petty crimes starting in 1947 for such insignificant crimes as stealing clothing and handbags.

Glover had always had troubled relationships with older women;

particularly his mother, Freda, and, later, his mother-in-law. Freda had a number of husbands and several boyfriends and he always harbored resentment toward his mother for leaving his father. When his mother died, Glover's "bizarre fascination with older women increased" as he was no longer satisfied by simply looking at them; he had an overwhelming urge to touch them. He was simultaneously fascinated and repulsed by nursing homes. When his mother-in-law was placed into such a home, he began to look forward to visiting her on Sunday afternoons because he now had a legitimate excuse to be in a nursing home. He often roamed around, looking for the oldest and most frail woman he could find and, whenever possible, he would indecently touch them. Their distress added to his excitement. This excitement of his was a symptom of gerontophilia; a sexual preference for the elderly and the opposite of pedophilia. Both were sexual paraphilias—abnormal and often extreme sexual desires.

In 1956, Glover relocated to Australia where he first resided in Melbourne and, in 1968, he settled in Mosman, Sydney. Shortly after moving to Australia he was convicted on two counts of larceny in Victoria, as well as another theft charge in New South Wales. In 1962, he was also convicted on two counts of assaulting women in Melbourne, two counts of indecent assault, four other counts of larceny, and another assault with bodily harm. Surprisingly he only received three years' probation for his offenses.

The attacks were reportedly quite severe and on each occasion the victim had certain articles of clothing removed. Victims were wrestled to the ground while Glover violently tore off their clothing. One victim was a 25-year-old woman who was on her way home one night at approximately 10:30 p.m. when she was followed and subsequently chased down a dark suburban street. She was knocked to the ground unconscious and later awakened in a garden bleeding profusely. Her undergarments were in "a state of disarray". Her assailant had run away when she had screamed and, thus, alerted residents in the area.

At the time of this attack, the 29-year-old Glover was employed for the Australian Broadcasting Company as a rigger while living in Camberwell, Melbourne.

In 1965, however, retribution finally caught up with Glover when he was convicted of being a Peeping Tom and was sentenced to three months in prison. He only served six weeks.

In 1968, Glover married the well-to-do middle-class Jacqueline Gail ("Gay") Rolls who he had met when he was working at a wine and spirits store in

Melbourne. She fell in love with him despite his being from a very poor working-class family and having arrived in Australia with only $3 (30 shillings) to his name. Gay's father, John Rolls, believed that the quiet, handsome young man was a good match for his beloved daughter. Whereas her mother thought the same in the beginning, she later decided that her future son-in-law had something to hide. Nevertheless, they gave the couple their blessings and Gay and Glover married soon thereafter and moved into her parents' comfortable house. The Glovers had two daughters: Kellie who was born in 1971; and Marney who came along in 1973. Later, a separate wing was added to the Rolls' house so the young family could have some privacy away from Essie's tyrannical nature.

In 1982, Glover's oft-married mother—now known as Freda Underwood—showed up on his doorstep. He loathed her almost as much as he despised his mother-in-law. His mother eventually died of breast cancer in 1988 in Gosford, 100 kilometers north of Sydney where Glover convinced her to move. After being diagnosed with the same cancer—which is rare in men—Glover underwent a mastectomy and then developed a prostate condition that rendered him sexually impotent.

Before he began killing in the late 1980s he had volunteered at the Senior Citizens Society and was considered among those who knew him as a trustworthy and friendly bloke.

Glover's family had no clue that he was the serial killer for whom the entire nation was looking. At this time he worked as a sales representative for Four 'n' Twenty Pies.

Prior to 1989, at the age of 56, when he allegedly started his murder spree (because there is some evidence that he may have been responsible for other murders committed prior to then), there was no proof that Glover had killed anyone up to that point. He had been married for 20 years when he started killing and in addition to having no clue about his predilections and murderous activities, his wife also had no knowledge of his previous convictions.

After each murder, Glover callously went about his life as normal.

The Crimes

Margaret Todhunter, 84

Before he began to kill, Glover had a "pre-murder" offense. On 11 January 1989, Glover witnessed 84-year-old Margaret Todhunter walking down Hale Road in Mosman. After he parked his vehicle he walked over to Todhunter, punched her in the face, and then stole the contents of her purse which included $209 that he spent at the Mosman RSL club, also called the Mosman Returned Servicemen's Club, on Military Road.

Investigators attributed the incident to a mugging and had little hope of finding out who the assailant was. Thankfully, she survived and only required eight stitches to close her head wound. Her description of her assailant would later prove pivotal in identifying Glover.

Gwendoline Mitchelhill, 82

On 1 March 1989, Glover was leaving the Mosman RSL when he saw 82-year-old Gwendoline Mitchelhill walking down the street toward her home in the upper middle-class suburb of Mosman. She lived in Camelia Gardens, an apartment block on Military Road where most of the residents were elderly widows even though there were also families and children.

Glover went to his car—a blue Falcon—removed a hammer, and hid it under his belt. He then followed Mitchelhill her entry door and as she opened it, he hit her on the back of her head with the hammer. He then continued to hit her with the hammer and his fists in her head and body, breaking several of her ribs.

Glover took Mitchelhill's purse which contained $100 and fled.

Two schoolboys exiting the elevator on the ground floor saw the victim attempting to crawl to the glass security doors at the front of the building with blood dripping from the serious wounds across her head. Her stockings had been torn from her legs and her cane and purse were laying further away. Her purse showed signs that someone had riffled through it. Other bystanders who came around to see what had happened, believing she had fallen and hit her head and, thus, paid no mind to the neat arrangement of her personal items. The boys quickly sought help.

There were no eyewitnesses to the actual attack or any clues or leads, nor was there any evidence to link this attack with Todhunter's earlier one. Compounding the problem was that good-hearted neighbors thought that Mitchelhill had simply fallen and, consequently, washed the crime scene of blood and any potential forensic evidence.

Police—not unlike Todhunter's assault—chalked this attack up as a mugging gone wrong.

Mitchelhill was rushed to the emergency room by ambulance and doctors worked quickly in an attempt to prevent further blood accumulation in her brain. During their examinations they decided that she simply had not fallen because her wounds were inconsistent with a fall. Instead, they determined that her head injuries, broken ribs, and dual black eyes suggested assault and contacted the Mosman police. Additionally, one of the ambulance medics told police of his concern regarding her purse that had been looked through but then placed neatly with the rest of her belongings. Later examination found that her wallet was not in her purse even though she did, in fact, have it earlier that day.

Unfortunately, Mitchelhill died that same evening.

A post-mortem examination the next day revealed "severe bruising to the right eye consistent with a fist, severe bruising to the right shoulder consistent with a blunt object, two wounds to back of the skull consistent with a blunt object, seven broken ribs consistent with a fist". The cause of death was attributed to her head and chest injuries which were determined to be consistent with a vicious attack. There was no evidence of sexual assault or other tampering.

Lady Winfreda Ashton, 84

On 9 May, Glover saw 84-year-old Lady Winfreda Ashton—the widow of renowned landscape painter Sir William Ashton—walking toward him on Military Road, on her way home to her Raglan Street residence. She kept her appointment at the Sydney eye hospital before going to the Mosman RSL until 2:30 p.m. She then stopped in to her local bank before proceeding to the nearby supermarket where she stopped to visit with friends. On her way home, she paused at her mailbox before heading toward the front entrance lobby of the building in which her unit was located.

Glover, donning a pair of gloves, followed her into her foyer where he attacked her with his hammer before throwing her to the ground and then dragging her into a trash bin alcove where he repeatedly bashed her head on the pavement. Glover later recalled that she had almost overpowered him, causing him to fall atop her, when he decided to hit her head on the pavement. Once she was unconscious, Glover removed her pantyhose and strangled her with them.

He then placed her shoes and cane by her feet and left with her purse which contained $100. Glover again went to the Mosman RSL where he commented to staff there that he "hoped that the sirens outside weren't for another mugging".

A neighbor found Ashton lying face-down diagonally across the concrete floor of the rubbish bin alcove with a pool of blood around her head. Her pantyhose were pulled so tightly around her neck that they had cut through her skin. She had a thin trickle of blood running from her mouth, her bare legs were crossed, and her arms were placed by her sides. Her cane and shoes were near her body and her purse had been opened, her wallet missing.

Detective Senior Constable Paul Mayger commented to his partner Detective Senior Constable Murray Byrnes that her murder had to have been committed by the same person who had already murdered once already and likely had assaulted another elderly woman.

At this point police believed that they may have a serial killer on the loose as all three victims thus far were wealthy elderly women who lived in the same area and were all assaulted or killed in the same manner before their purses were stolen. Ashton's injuries paralleled Mitchelhill's. The two crime scenes were only approximately one kilometer apart and both murder victims were killed at the entrance to their residences.

Ashton's autopsy was conducted by Argentinian-born Dr. Liliana Schwartz and this was her first homicide as a forensic pathologist in Australia. Schwartz checked the victim's body temperature, the extent of rigor mortis, and whether there were any signs of sexual assault; the latter which she determined did not occur as there was no evidence of semen. The ligature mark around her neck measured nine centimeters and she had bruising on her nose, the side of her head, her neck, and upon both eyelids. She had also bitten her lip at some point which caused damage to the inside of her mouth. She had an open wound on her cheek that had a small, semicircular abrasion near it.

As the victim still had her diamond ring on, robbery was not considered the primary motive even though her purse was taken.

The police, led by Detective Mike Hagan, sought to create a profile of the killer. They consulted with Dr. Rod Milton, a forensic psychiatrist whose profile was not released to the public.

On 9 July, Ashton's purse was found, interestingly, in Ashton Park and the woman who found the purse did not realize its significance, put it in Ashton's mailbox as stated on the papers inside of it, thus likely destroying any potential evidence that may have been on or inside the purse.

Other crimes (not murders)

On 6 June, Glover molested 77-year-old Marjorie Moseley at the Wesley Gardens Retirement Home in Belrose. She told staff that a man had put his hand under her nightgown; however, she could not identify her assailant.

Later that month, on 24 June, Glover lifted the dress of an elderly female patient at the Caroline Chisholm Nursing Home in Lane Cove and fondled her buttocks. In an adjoining room, he slid his hand down the front of another patient's nightgown and caressed her breasts. The second woman cried for help and Glover was questioned briefly before leaving.

On 8 August, Effie Carnie was assaulted on a back street in Lindfield, in Sydney's upper North Shore.

On 6 October, Glover pretended to be a physician and ran his hand up blind patient Phyllis McNeil's dress at the Wybenia Nursing Home in Neutral Bay in the lower North Shore area. McNeil called for help and Glover was neither suspected of nor identified as her molester.

Later that month on 18 October, Glover followed 86-year-old widow Doris Cox as she walked down Spit Road to her retirement village in Mosman. In a secluded stairwell at the front of the building he slammed her face into a brick wall where she fell to the ground. She was found sitting on the ground, calling for help with her face covered in blood, several scrapes on her face, and missing a few of her teeth. Luckily, Cox survived; however, she could not provide a clear description of her attacker or provide a clear recollection of what happened, likely due to her dementia. Again, neighbors washed down the area before investigators arrived, thus destroying any potential forensic evidence.

The medical examiner who conducted the autopsies on the first two victims examined Cox's injuries and concluded that they were consistent with being attacked in a similar fashion.

Margaret Pahud, 78

On 2 November, Glover approached 78-year-old Dorothy Benke while she was walking home on a backstreet just off Longueville Road in Lane Cove that was approximately ten kilometers from Mosman. He was en route to Kamilaroi Retirement Centre when he spotted Benke, for whom he offered to carry her groceries home. While initially hesitant, Benke thought that the likely 65-year-old man had a pleasant face. The talked as they walked and when they reached her house, she decided he looked harmless enough and invited him into her house for a cup of tea; however, Glover declined the tea and left, having decided that he didn't want to harm her.

After Glover left Benke's house he passed 85-year-old Margaret Pahud on her way home—also struggling with heavy grocery bags. Anger and hatred welled within him as he attacked her from behind, hitting her in the head with his hammer. She fell, face-down at his feet and he hit her again. He pulled at her dress, exposing her left breast and shoulder and then, upon hearing the sound of children's voices approaching, grabbed her purse and walked away.

This time police were certain that her assault was the work of the now-dubbed "Granny Killer" as she was hit on the back of her head with a blunt instrument and after collapsing was again struck on the side of her head. Her clothing, shoes, and cane were arranged and her handbag had been taken.

Again, there were no witnesses;

however, not long after her assault a young schoolgirl found her body, thinking at first that it was simply a pile of clothing. She alerted her mother and another neighbor who rushed to the scene. Pahud was lying face-down with her head surrounded by a large pool of blood. One neighbor ran to a nearby doctor's office to seek help; however, when the physician arrived he pronounced Pahud dead.

And again, neighbors washed down the crime scene.

This time, the victim's entire purse was missing.

While the police were en route, Glover had stopped on the grounds of a nearby golf club and went through Pahud's purse. He then went to the Mosman RSL Club to spend the $300 he had stolen.

Olive Cleveland, 81

A mere 24 hours after he murdered Pahud, Glover struck up a conversation with 81-year-old Olive Cleveland as she was sitting on a bench just outside the Wesley Gardens Retirement Village (where Glover had molested Marjorie Mosely) in Belrose. At some point Cleveland became uncomfortable and got up to walk to the main building; however, Glover grabbed her from behind and forced her down a ramp into a secluded side lane where he hit her and repeatedly bashed her head into the concrete before removing her pantyhose and strangling her with them. Like the other victims, Glover rearranged her clothing, shoes, glasses, and cane and left with $60 stolen from her purse.

She was found lying face-down across the pathway and this time the killer added to his signature by pulling up her dress to expose her legs. Her pantyhose had been removed and were tied tightly around her throat, and her head was surrounded by a pool of blood.

Not unlike some of Glover's earlier victims, Cleveland's injuries were originally attributed to a fall and the crime scene was, again, washed down before police and ambulance arrived. Also again, there were no eyewitnesses.

The autopsy was eerily similar to the others. Bruising and lacerations around the head and body with cause of death attributed to strangling by her pantyhose which were tied around her neck three times.

At this point police were starting to assemble clues about the killer. To this point he always struck at around 3:00 p.m. and there were never any witnesses to the actual assaults.

The state government offered a $200,000 reward for any information about the "Granny Killer".

Muriel Falconer, 93

On 23 November, Glover was sitting in the Buena Vista Hotel on Middle Head

Road in Mosman drinking a beer when he glimpsed 93-year-old widow Muriel Falconer walking across the street. Falconer was still rather active and spry for her age and she was returning from the local fruit shop, bank, other errands, and had just collected her "Meals on Wheels." It was around 5:00 p.m. Glover could feel the rage and contempt welling up inside of him.

He left his beer half-full and went to his car that he audaciously parked opposite the police station to retrieve his gloves and hammer and then followed Falconer to the exterior of her Muston Street home. From behind, he placed his hand around her mouth to silence her and then repeatedly hit her in the head and neck with his hammer.

When she fell, Glover began to remove her pantyhose; however, Falconer regained consciousness and cried for help which forced Glover to continue to hit her with the hammer until she finally stopped resisting. He removed her undergarments and strangled her with them before searching her purse and house for valuables. After rearranging her shoes, he left with $100 in stolen money.

Her body was discovered the next day by a neighbor who entered with a spare key after Meals on Wheels had not been able to get a hold of Falconer at both 11:30 a.m. and again at 1:00 p.m. The neighbor saw Falconer lying face-down in the hallway, naked from the waist down, her dress and petticoat pulled above her head, and a large pool of blood streaming from her wounds. Her shoes and bags were arranged neatly near her feet and her purse was open.

This time, however, the crime scene was intact and forensic evidence to include bloody shoeprints was able to be collected. These prints would later match Glover's shoes.

Falconer's autopsy revealed similar afflictions as the other victims of the "Granny Killer." She had been beaten, her head was fractured in three places, her face contained a number of broken bones, and her pantyhose and dress belt were wrapped tightly around her throat.

A neighbor identified the attacker as "middle-aged, portly, and grey-haired"— someone who would fit in easily into the Mosman area. The reward was increased to $250,000 by Christmas.

The task force decided to check all nearby police stations for any records of attacks upon elderly women. One report was particularly interesting: that of Margaret Todhunter who had been attacked by a grey-haired man who was "50 years of age, well-kept, broad shoulders, thick chest, large stomach, and who wore a white business shirt and cream trousers" who grabbed her bag. This description fit Glover to a tee.

Daisy Roberts, 82 (not murdered)

After Muriel Falconer's murder, Glover visited the Greenwich Hospital on River Road on one of his pie sales rounds on 11 January 1990. He entered the hospital's palliative care ward where he found four elderly, ill women including 82-year-old advanced cancer patient Daisy Roberts (who has since passed away). While in his work uniform and carrying a clipboard, Glover asked Roberts if she "was losing any body heat" before pulling up her nightgown and "touch[ing] her in an indecent manner".

Roberts called for help and this time hospital sister Pauline Davis saw Glover in the ward. She confronted him and he ran; however, Davis was able to record his car's license number and called the police. This time, also, hospital staff was able to both name and identify Glover as he was already known from his pie rounds.

One week later the police returned with a photograph of Glover and both Davis and Roberts were able to positively identify him. While this was, indeed, a significant breakthrough, the hospital assaults were not as of yet linked to the "Granny Killer" murders. Compounding the problem was that said assaults were not reported to the murder task force for three weeks.

Instead, detectives from Chatswood Police Station contacted Glover and requested he attend an interview at the station the following day. Of course, he failed to appear and police subsequently called his home and were informed by his wife that he had attempted suicide via overdose and was recovering at the Royal North Shore Hospital. At the hospital, Glover declined to be interviewed; however, he did permit police to take a Polaroid photograph of him. This was the photo that police had shown to Davis and Roberts.

Hospital staff also handed the police a handwritten suicide note from Glover on a sheet of Four 'n' Twenty Pies letterhead that said, "no more grannies … grannies" and "Essie started it"—Essie being Glover's mother-in-law, Veronica Rolls, who had lived with her daughter and son-in-law for 13 years before moving into a nursing home in 1988. She ultimately died on 21 January 1989. Glover's own mother had also recently passed away on 11 October 1988. Experts believe that these deaths were a catalyst for his murders in addition to a deep-seated hatred of his mother for leaving his father and remarrying coupled with an equally intense hatred of his mother-in-law.

It took two more weeks before the note and the photo were given to the task force assembled to catch Australia's first serial killer.

Glover was interviewed over the nursing home assaults and denied all accusations. Since police had limited evidence they decided not to question him about the murders because, they believed, that it would make Glover aware of police suspicions against him. Instead, he was placed under constant surveillance with an automatic tracking device. To evade potential followers, Glover would drive around the block more than once or drive the wrong way up one-way streets. Had the police done their job properly, Glover's last victim might still be alive today.

Joan Sinclair, 60

Glover's last victim was 60-year-old divorcee Joan Sinclair from Beauty Point, Mosman, with whom Glover had been having a relationship. On 19 March 1990, while police had him under surveillance, he went to visit his lover who let him into her home at approximately 10:00 a.m. By 1:00 p.m. there had been no sign of Glover or any movement inside of the house.

Later in the afternoon two boys attempted to enter the house but the gate was locked. They sought assistance from a neighbor to no avail. Additionally, a dog barking inside the house indicated something was not quite right. At approximately 5:00 p.m., the surveillance team became concerned and obtained permission to enter the house at 6:00 p.m.

Two uniformed officers knocked on the front door to no avail. They saw through the rear glass door a hammer lying in a pool of dried blood atop a mat. Four detectives searched the house and found Sinclair's battered head wrapped in a bundle of blood-slaked towels. She was nude from the waist down and her pantyhose were tied around her neck. This time, her genitals showed signs of damage; however, Glover denied sexually assaulting her.

After finding Sinclair's body they searched for Glover who was later discovered unconscious in a filled bathtub. He was transported to Royal North Shore Hospital and placed under police guard.

Sinclair's cause of death was due to multiple head wounds from the claw hammer found at the scene. Despite some dissimilarities between her murder and the other murders, police believed there was ample evidence to suggest that they were all linked and that Glover was the perpetrator.

Glover told police he murdered Sinclair and explained their relationship which he claimed had been ongoing for some time. He admitted to beating her head with his hammer, removing her pantyhose, and strangling her with them. He then admitted to rolling her body onto a mat before wrapping four towels around her head to reduce the blood flow, and then dragging her lifeless body across the floor. He then claimed to have run the bath and taken a handful of Valium with a bottle of Vat 69 before slashing his left wrist and lying down in the bath to die. Police were, in fact, relieved that Glover lived so they wouldn't have to speculate forever as to whether he was the "Granny Killer" or not.

Investigation and Arrest

By January 1990, Glover had been on his murderous rampage for ten months and had already murdered five elderly women and assaulted several more in hospitals and nursing homes. Each victim had been attacked within a few kilometers of the Greenwich Hospital, and one had been murdered a mere 250 meters from the hospital's front gate.

As previously mentioned, despite

assemblage of a massive police task force consisting of 70 officers the previous November to catch Australia's first serial killer, alarm bells failed to go off when police botched their chance to question Glover and obtain a search warrant for his house and car. Had they obtained a warrant, they would have discovered the gloves and hammer under his front seat. Instead, police called Glover to ask him to come in for an interview on 13 January.

Thus, police have been subject to scathing criticisms from a number of sources because had they acted in a timely manner then Sinclair might still be alive today.

When confronted with the evidence

against him, Glover admitted to the murders; however, he denied responsibility for other crimes in which he was the prime suspect such as the 1977 murder of Florence Broadhurst in Paddington.

In sum, he was charged with 14 offenses: six counts of first-degree murder, one count of attempted murder, one count of robbery with wounding, one count of robbery, four counts of indecent assault, and one count of assaulting a female.

Trial and Conviction

Glover's trial began on 28 March 1990 in which he pled not guilty on the grounds of diminished responsibility.

One psychiatrist who evaluated Glover testified that he had built up hostility and aggression against his mother since he was a child, and then against his mother-in-law who was called his "trigger". When his mother-in-law died, Glover felt he had to take out his aggression against a surrogate. The psychiatrist also stated that the very few mass murderers in Australia are perpetrated by mentally ill perpetrators who oftentimes have some organic brain disease; however, at the time of his crimes Glover was completely sane. He was described as an anger-retaliatory predator with narcissistic tendencies despite outwardly being a "nice guy" with a "normal" life.

Thus, the prosecutor maintained throughout the trial that Glover was, indeed, fully aware of his actions because when he killed his victims he was planning how he would spend the victims' money, not to mention that he took time to clean his hammer with acid to destroy any potential biological evidence. As Glover was impotent and had zero interest in sex, his ritualistic strangulation of his victims with pantyhose was done to trick the police into thinking that the murderer was sexually motivated.

Compounding the problem was that Glover was seriously addicted to poker machines and the best way for him to obtain more money with which to gamble was to steal it.

On 29 November 1990, Glover was found guilty and after the verdict was delivered, presiding Judge James Wood stressed Glover's dangerousness. He said, "[Glover] is able to choose when to attack and when to stay his hand. He is cunning and able to cover his tracks. It is plain that he has chosen his moments carefully. Although the crimes have been opportunistic, he has not gone in where the risks were overwhelming".

Wood added that Glover's crimes involved "extreme violence inflicted on elderly women, accompanied by theft or robbery of their property" thus making Glover "exceedingly dangerous" and this opinion was mirrored by the psychiatrists who proffered testimony at his trial.

Sentence

Thus, due to Wood's sentiments attesting to Glover's dangerousness, he said, "I have no alternative other than to impose the maximum available sentence, which means that the prisoner will be required to spend the remainder of his natural life in Jail. It is inappropriate to express any date as to release on parole. Having regard to those life sentences, this is not a case where the prisoner may ever be released pursuant to order of this court. He is never to be released".

After being sentenced to life without

any possibility of parole, Glover expressed that his only concern was that he would never see the ocean again. He failed to demonstrate much emotion as Wood handed down his sentence.

Aftermath

After his convictions, Glover admitted that he "never worried about who his victims were, or why he killed them" and that he wanted to stop but could not.

Glover committed suicide in prison by hanging himself (his third known attempt). The 72-year-old "Granny Killer" was found hanging from a shower rail in his cell in Lithgow Prison in New South Wales.

Prior to doing so, he handed his last visitor a sketch of a park with a number of changes in the sketch which Glover pointed out. In the sketch were two palm trees; in the middle of the right one was the number "nine" composed of leaves and branches. The number nine is said to represent the number of murders that Glover committed—or the number of unsolved murders he likely also committed. The nine additional victims/ unsolved cases include: Elsie Boyes, 63, 3 June 1967, in Prahran; Emmie May Anderson, 78, 19 October 1961, in East Melbourne; Irene Kiddle, 61, 22 March 1963, in Saint Kilda; Christina Yankos, 63, 9 April 1968, in Albert Park; Florence Broadhurst, 78, 16 October

1977, in Paddington; Josephine McDonald, 72, 29 August 1984, in Ettalong; Wanda Amundsen, 83, 21 November 1986, in Umina; as well as two other unknown victims.

THE STRANGE DISAPPEARANCE OF PATRICIA MEEHAN

NATHAN NIXON

Patricia Meehan Disappearance

The story of Patricia Meehan is a very strange and puzzling one. She seemingly disappeared into the night with little reason. The case has remained unsolved since 1989. With few witnesses, the full events are sketchy at best. What is well known about this case is that our culture has seemingly thought of every possible scenario to explain what happened to her. To understand and possibly solve the case, understanding the person that Patricia Meehan was is of paramount importance.

Patricia Meehan was never afraid of change. Her path of life took her all over the United States and to nearly every type of region. She was born on November 1, 1951 in Pittsburgh, Pennsylvania. She lived a typical life. She was said to have been "the perfect child" by her loving parents and by all who knew her. She had great ambition to see the world and to attack life with a smile. Socially she was on the same level as her peers. When she decided to attend college in Oklahoma City, Oklahoma, no one was really surprised. That was who Patricia was. That is exactly what she did.

She studied early childhood development and earned her degree in four years of college study. Again, she was living the American dream and successfully setting up a future to thrive. She made many friends in Oklahoma, even though it was a foreign place to a young woman from Pittsburgh. She took up a career in early childhood caregiving in Oklahoma and thrived in the profession for nearly 10 years. She was unhappy, or perhaps, unfulfilled in her work. She sporadically spoke with her family and a few friends from back home in Pennsylvania at the time. People knew Patricia to take risks. She was never afraid to change her outlook if it meant a new adventure or perhaps a new challenge lay ahead. In 1985, she made a major life change that would, effectively, lead to her ultimate disappearance.

She had informed her parents in the years prior that she wanted to become involved in animal care. She made this a reality when she moved to Bozeman, Montana in 1985. She moved alone. Patricia was not married and had left her simple, safe life behind in Oklahoma to pursue a career as a ranch hand. While this major career shift was motivated to start a happier life, it ultimately didn't always pay the bills. She worked numerous odd-jobs in the industry and could successfully make ends meet on her own. She continued this new lifestyle for four years in Bozeman, Montana.

The last person that can be fully confirmed to have seen Patricia Meehan alive was her landlord. Meehan's landlord reported to police investigators later that she seemed much more hyper than normal. This struck the landlord as extremely odd for the normally mellow, collected Patricia. Nonetheless, there were absolutely no problems between the two in any way. Patricia always paid her rent and was an "overall great tenant" to have.

The evening of April 20, 1989 is one of great speculation as to what really happened. The testimony of Peggy Bueller has always been a key component to the theories of Patricia's disappearance.

At approximately 8:05 P.M. Peggy Bueller and her

father were traveling west bound on Montana State Highway 200. They were passing through the tiny town of Circle, Montana. To their surprise, they could see a set of vehicle headlights heading straight at them up ahead. A vehicle heading east was driving on the wrong side of the road. Peggy managed to swerve onto the shoulder and avoid a head-on collision with the opposing driver. The car that had been following behind Peggy was driven by an off-duty police dispatcher named Carol Heitz. Unfortunately for Carol, she was not able to swerve and avoid a collision.

Peggy Bueller had pulled over and gazed in her rear-view mirror in time to see the collision with the car driven by Carol Heitz. Thankfully, no injuries occurred in the accident. The story is very odd and somewhat eerie from this point. Just after impact, Carol Heitz emerged from her vehicle unharmed. She was shook up, but suffered no major injury. Being a police dispatcher, her first concern was for the other driver. The car that was traveling east bound was driven by Patricia Meehan. Patricia was next to emerge from her car after the impact. She stood in the middle of the road, and proceeded to slowly approach the car of Carol Heitz. According to Heitz, Patricia Meehan did not utter a single word. "She approached me calmly and silently," Heitz reported. "She seemingly stared directly through me from the moment she began to approach me."

Peggy Bueller remained in her vehicle and observed what was taking place. What she observed was "one of the strangest acts" she had ever seen. Peggy and Heitz agree that Patricia climbed over a fence just off of the road after she passed by Carol. She took only a step after getting over the fence and turned back around to stare upon the accident. She made no noise or any sort of expression. She stood there for at least two minutes. Heitz described Meehan as someone who seemed to be observing the accident scene rather than someone who had been involved in the accident. After a few short minutes, Meehan turned around and walked into a secluded Montana field into the pitch dark night. This was the last confirmed sighting of Patricia Meehan. By the time police arrived to sort out the accident, the whereabouts of Patricia were unknown. Peggy and Carol gave the exact same story in separate interviews with investigators. As eerie as the accident had unfolded, it had ended quietly and abruptly. Patricia Meehan was officially gone.

Peggy Bueller quickly drove into town when Patricia disappeared into the night. Her father stayed with Carol Heitz at the scene of the accident. Peggy reached a phone within ten minutes and alerted the authorities. When police arrived, an extensive search of the field where Patricia was seen walking away to turned up nothing. It only took police 15 minutes to identify the then mystery woman as Patricia Meehan after they ran the license plate of the vehicle. She was a registered member of the Bozeman, Montana community and had no criminal record. This was shocking to police who had assumed the woman left due to the fact that police would be arriving to the scene to investigate the accident. This posed the burning question that is still unanswered of why this woman would leave the scene of the accident if she had no criminal record.

Police made efforts to investigate the field immediately following the accident. Police discovered a tennis shoe about a mile into the field that had been accompanying a trail of footprints. The shoe matched what would have been the approximate size of the foot of Patricia Meehan. Oddly enough, the tracks seemingly disappear. Due to darkness, the investigation was suspended until the following morning of April 21. When police arrived to further check for a trail, the footprints led to nothing. The terrain had an influence in this as well as the fact that the actual shoe prints were gone, likely due to Patricia going barefoot at this point in her walk. Police had no leads.

There were two major theories that investigators had arrived at to this point. The first was the most likely. They believed that Patricia had hitchhiked from a small rural road in the area with a trucker. This could obviously not be confirmed, however the lack of a body, further clothes or footprints, as well as a lack of any whereabouts in surrounding cities points to this to be the likely case. The second theory they had suggest that she stowed away in a hay truck in the area and accomplished the same thing. This proved later to be unlikely as no hay trucks were confirmed to be in the field or in the immediate area.

    The Meehan family arrived to Montana from Pittsburgh in the day following the accident. They distributed over 2,000 missing person flyers in the surrounding Montana towns and provided police with valuable information. The flyers turned up numerous calls, however none of these would lead to finding Patricia. Over 500 local volunteers searched the mountainous terrain around the accident site in an effort to possibly locate Patricia. For days, people walked the area. Some even brought dogs to perhaps catch a scent trail. These searches turned up absolutely nothing. There was no evidence of human activity in the mountains, and there were no evidence of a body or struggle in the surrounding area. Patricia had seemingly disappeared without a trace after taking a path into a secluded field. Perhaps the events in the days and weeks prior could shed some light into who Patricia was and things she had been recently going through.

    The Meehan family revealed to police that Patricia had been going through some dark times in the past couple of months. Patricia was somewhat at a dead end and was feeling lost. She had asked her parents if she could return home in an effort to get back on track. Her parent's agreed, but only if she see a psychologist leading to coming home. Patricia agreed. She was diagnosed as suffering from depression. Ironically, she had an appointment with her psychologist the morning after the accident on April 21. She obviously never made this appointment.

Police also were suspicious as to why Patricia was even in this part of the state anyway. She had an appointment in Bozeman, Montana for the next morning. Bozeman was where she was living. The direction of travel she was taking at the time of the accident was in the opposite direction of Bozeman. Investigators asked the Meehan family if they had any idea where she may be going or what she was doing in this remote part of Montana. They had absolutely no idea. It was evident to police that she had no intention of returning to Bozeman to make her appointment the next morning. But could there be more to this part of the story?

The Meehan family had a roll of film developed that had been found in Patricia's car the night of the accident. The film was fully used. There were numerous pictures of nature. Beautiful countryside and the secluded area that Patricia loved. There were also numerous pictures of animals, specifically horses, that Patricia had devoted her life to in the recent years.

Patricia's family stumbled across one picture that was quite alarming. A random picture that Patricia had taken in front of a mirror. She had a very confused look on her face and seemed lost. Investigation of the picture by mental professionals led some to believe she could have been suffering from amnesia. This could obviously not be proven, but would go further in explaining the odd behavior she displayed that night. Some of the investigators pointed to this as a possible reason that she was driving away from Bozeman and was 300 miles away from home. Could she simply have forgotten how to get home? Could her mental health had gotten that bad?

Patricia had been driving on the wrong side of the road and made no effort to swerve. Police drew two possible conclusions to this fact. The first was that she was so far lost in amnesia that she simply didn't think she was doing anything wrong or perhaps forgot the basic rules of driving. The second was that she was possibly trying to harm herself or had gotten so careless that the results were not clearly thought through. These are obviously speculation and will never be proven one way or the other. The mental health of Patricia was most assuredly in a low place.

The roll of film that was developed also proved something else to investigators and the Meehan family. Socially, she was in a dark place also. Out of every picture that had been developed, not one of them featured people that weren't named Patricia Meehan. This is clearly not the norm. Patricia had mentioned that she had had a few boyfriends since arriving in Montana, but nothing serious and committal. She had previously mentioned to her parents that she had become lonely and never really made any friends in her new home. This could help to explain the depression and possible mental health issues that she had developed.

Over the last 25 years, there have been over 5,000 reported sightings of Patricia Meehan. Through all of this, only 3 of those do police feel could be Patricia or are even likely to be her. In the days following her disappearance, there were some interesting leads that were generated by the public calls on the missing person flyers.

On May 4, 1989 just two weeks after the accident, a strong lead was generated out of Luverne, Minnesota. Out of all of the possible sightings, this is considered by police and those surrounding the case to be the most likely sighting of Patricia. A police officer in Luverne claimed to have seen Patricia sitting in a Hardee's restaurant by herself. For over five hours, she was sitting in corner booth drinking water. She remained until closing time, and then proceeded to walk to a nearby 24 hour diner. Here, the officer questioned her. The woman refused adamantly to give her name. She first said that she was from Colorado, and later said she was from Israel. The major problem with all of this is that the officer could not detain her. She had done nothing wrong. However, he left without further checking to identify her. This was perhaps the best chance to obtain Patricia if this indeed was her. The officer left and where this mystery woman went next is unknown.

Another interesting sighting occurred on May 19, 1989. This is nearly one full month after the accident. A waitress at a local restaurant in Bozeman, Montana reported seeing Patricia eating there. She informed police that Patricia at in a hurry and said she had to go shopping at 9 A.M. She said she was polite, but did seem to be displaying odd behavior. Another waitress on the same shift also reported seeing her. This waitress said she was talking to herself and seemed disoriented. Patricia left the restaurant and again, no attempts were really made to investigate who she really was.

The theories that surround this case are perhaps the most interesting in the current media. If Patricia was alive today, she would be in her late 60's. This would obviously make her hard to identify in the general public. This leads to the first theory.

The first, and generally most believed theory, is that Patricia simply wanted another fresh start. She had done this in the past, albeit in a much less drastic way.

She wanted a fresh start after high school, so she attended college in Oklahoma City, Oklahoma. She wanted a career change and a change of passion nearly 10 years after she started her career, so she moved to Bozeman, Montana and became a ranch hand. Many feel that she again wanted a career change and a life change at this point in her life. Turning to her parents, they gave her an ultimatum to see a psychologist before she came home. The theory suggest that she wasn't happy with her family about this. She obtained her fresh start by planning an event that would allow her to vanish into the unknown. What better place to accomplish this than a secluded highway in rural Montana where she could simply walk away.

This theory goes on further to explain that she had walked across the field and met up with someone who would drive her away. This theory doesn't sound too crazy at this juncture. The who or why is unknown, but the basis of the theory is mostly sound. Where she would have started this new life is completely unknown. But for a person who was struggling socially, not completely happy, and perhaps not enjoying the rural life as much as she had anticipated, this theory makes some sense.

The second popular theory is the more logical, medically supported theory. The collision that Patricia Meehan had was significant. While there were no injuries on the exterior, a concussion is without a doubt a possibility of this type of vehicle accident. Some believe that it was not amnesia to blame, but a concussion that would cause her to act so disoriented after the accident. The theory suggest that she exited her vehicle with a head injury and collapsed in the field shortly after beginning her walk into the night.

Montana is home to vast amounts of wildlife and has a very abstract climate. The night time temperatures in April in Montana typically are going to approach freezing. Anything under 50 degrees at altitude is going to be a severe situation for a minimally clothed, small woman with a possible head injury. The theory suggest that she was unconscious overnight and perhaps was eaten by animals, which would explain the lack of a body or any other evidence to her disappearance. It is for this reason that the theory is typically not accepted. Even with this, there would have been signs of this happening by one of the numerous volunteers or investigators in the following days.

The disappearance of Patricia Meehan has garnered national attention for the past 25 years. On November 1, 1989 the case was featured on *Unsolved Mysteries*. This would have marked the 38th birthday for Patricia.

Sightings are still reported on Patricia and a host

of other in the United States. With each passing year, it is all too assuring that this case will never be solved. The lack of information on the case is puzzling. Those who choose to research the case will find that there is little information beyond the night of the accident and some significant reported sightings. All of these factors have led to a disappearance that has stumped police since that fateful night.

      Patricia Meehan was an ambitious woman. She took risk in efforts to accomplish her goals and to get the most out of life. Anyone who ever knew her would say that she was a wonderful person with a positive view of the world. She loved her family dearly, and she loved her life deeply. She confidently left home to discover new opportunities on multiple occasions. It seems that life perhaps got too much for her in Montana. Maybe she just wanted to come home. Whatever the case, Patricia Meehan disappeared in April 1989, and has yet to be found. This beautiful young woman hasn't officially turned up in over 25 years. This tragic case may never be closed. A sure fact of the case is that Patricia was a sweet woman who didn't get in this situation by means of risky behavior or negative interactions. Likely, her disappearance can be attributed to a social low spot where she needed help that she didn't go through with getting. Maybe one day the truth of where her walk ultimately led will come out.

THE DISAPPEAR-ANCE OF KELSIE SCHELLING

ANA BENSON

Every time a woman goes missing or is found

murdered, the police usually takes a closer look at their spouses or boyfriends. It is a standard procedure, especially if there were indications that they were in a troubled relationship. The disappearance of Kelsie Schelling is one of the biggest mysteries in Colorado. This young pregnant woman was last seen in February of 2013 and the case is still open to this day.

However, Kelsie's family was quite disappointed at the lack of interest by the police to investigate her then-boyfriend Donthe Lucas, who was clearly involved in this crime. After all, Donthe did invite Kelsie to his hometown on that fateful night and he was the last person who saw her alive. When they realized that the police are stalling with the investigation, the family made a promise that Kelsie's case will not be forgotten until they discover what really happened. They kept the public informed through their Facebook page and eventually managed to reach the Colorado Bureau of Investigation.

Early life

Kelsie Jean Schelling was born on 18th February 1991 in Holyoke, Colorado. She grew up in a tightknit family and later became even closer to her mother after the divorce of her parents. Kelsie was only eleven years old when they split up but she would often talk to her father as well. However, they didn't see each other that often because he moved to a different part of town. After graduating from high school, Kelsie attended Northeastern Junior College located in Sterling, Colorado. She was fascinated with psychology and planned to major in it once she gets accepted to the university.

Kelsie was friendly and outspoken, so it comes as no surprise that she had many friends and was a life of every party. During her time at Northeastern Junior College, Kelsie met Donthe Lucas. He was a star player on the basketball team and the two of them fell in love instantly. Donthe Lucas had a very difficult childhood and he grew up in Pueblo, Colorado which is an infamous place known for higher crime rates than anywhere else in the state. He loved basketball and it was clear that he would be an outstanding athlete even in high school. Basketball players do have enormous salaries so Donthe Lucas did see it as an opportunity to help his family out further down the line.

He was hoping that a scout would attend one of his games and recruit him for one of bigger colleges or universities that had a good basketball team. But his big break never happened. Instead, he ended up in Northeastern Junior College which was alright, but Donthe wasn't quite happy with that outcome. His dissatisfaction was evident even in the relationship with Kelsie. Their romance had constant ups and downs, and the two of them would break up, and get back together which drove Kelsie mad. They did finally call it quits after several semesters, and didn't see each other for quite some time.

After finishing the two years at the junior college, Kelsie pursued her education even further, and she moved to California to attend Vanguard University in Costa Mesa. She was finally able to study psychology full time. Donthe continued to play basketball for Emporia State University in Kansas. Kelsie's family was happy she managed to end her relationship with the troubled basketball player, and they hoped that she would make a new life far away from Colorado. Kelsie was independent and she enjoyed living and studying in California. When she wasn't attending classes, Kelsie worked at a tanning salon with her best friend. However, she did drop out of the college because the school work was a bit too much for her at the time and her only option was to go back home. She moved to Denver in 2012 and started working in a store. Meanwhile, Donthe Lucas was back in his hometown Pueblo.

The two of them started talking once again during

the autumn of 2012. It was obvious that they still had feelings for each other, so no one was surprised when Donthe and Kelsie decided to spend the Christmas holidays together. The couple seemed happy to everyone around them, but Kelsie did tell her friends that their relationship was still very toxic. Donthe was still treating her badly, calling her names, and starting unnecessary fights. Soon enough everything will change. A few weeks after the holidays, Kelsie found out that she was pregnant. Shocked at first, Kelsie was lost and decided not to tell anyone for a couple of weeks. But keeping a secret was hard. So she called her mother and told her the news. Kelsie's mother Laura would later say that even though her daughter felt a bit stressed, she was still excited about the pregnancy. Yes, she was young but Kelsie was determined to make it work.

    Donthe Lucas didn't take the news so well. Having in mind how dissatisfied he felt about his failed basketball career, it is not wrong to assume that the news about a baby simply solidified the fact that his dreams will never come true. Kelsie noticed the change in his mood and openly told him that he doesn't have to be a part of their baby's life. But it is also worth mentioning that Kelsie confided in her best friend that Donthe was ecstatic to become a father at one point. However, his mind was constantly changing. Kelsie went to see her doctor on 4th of February 2013 and he confirmed that she was eight weeks pregnant. The baby was healthy and doing well. The doctor provided her with an ultrasound of the unborn baby, and she was full of joy. Kelsie immediately sent out the pictures to her mother, her friends, and Donthe. Unfortunately, the excitement will not last forever.

The night of the disappearance

Donthe and Kelsey exchanged several emails on

February 3rd, 2013. He invited her to visit him in Pueblo.

She turned him down saying that she needs to go for a checkup the next day to make sure everything is alright with the baby. After seeing her doctor on the morning of February 4th, 2013, Kelsie went straight to the store. She worked the second shift and was expected to come home sometime after 10:00 PM that night. However, she was in contact with Donthe for the entire day, texting back and forth about the pregnancy. Donthe told her that she should drive out to Pueblo after work because he had a surprise for her. Not knowing what it is, Kelsie asked for more information because Pueblo is two hours away from Denver, and she would probably be tired after work. He insisted that she would be happy with his surprise and that he cannot tell her anything over the phone.

It is safe to assume that Kelsie thought that Donthe was ready to change and start a family with her. Their relationship wasn't a standard one but it seemed like Kelsie was willing to move past all the negative things and focus on the future. So after her shift ended, Kelsie got in her Chevy Cruze LTZ and drove to Pueblo in the middle of the night. Donthe was supposed to meet her in a parking lot in front of a local Walmart. The surveillance cameras did confirm that Kelsie got there on time, but Donthe was nowhere to be seen. She waited in a parked car for almost an hour before sending another text message to Donthe, saying that she has been in the parking lot for too long and that she would come pick him up at whatever location he is at the moment. She got a reply sometime around 12:15 AM.

Donthe told her that he will be waiting for her in the street next to his grandmother's home. Kelsie is seen exiting the parking lot a couple of minutes after she got the message. She clearly did arrive at the second rendezvous spot, but once again Donthe wasn't there. Kelsie sent him another message asking where is he and Donthe replied that he will be there in a minute. This is the last known communication between these two until sometime before 04:00 AM. After going through the phone records, police did discover that Donthe called Kelsie at 03:54 AM but she didn't pick up. The significance of this mysterious phone call will be revealed later. After reviewing the cell tower pings for both phones, the investigators did discover that they were in close proximity to each other.

The search for Kelsie

Kelsie's mother Laura got really worried the next day because she wasn't able to reach her daughter over the phone. She tried calling numerous times but it went straight to the voicemail. The last message she got from her daughter was the ultrasound image of her unborn child, and Laura wasn't sure if something happened to Kelsie after work, or she was ignoring her calls. Laura contacted Kelsie's friends who told her that she went to Pueblo to meet with Donthe. With no word from her daughter, she called Donthe who picked up his phone and told Laura that he had seen Kelsie last night, but that she drove back home in the morning.

Laura was starting to panic, but she did tell Donthe that she would involve the police if she doesn't hear from her daughter soon. Laura and Kelsie were very close and they did tell each other everything, but she suspected that her daughter kept this information from her because she didn't want Laura to know that she was meeting with Donthe. After all, Laura was aware of the nature of their relationship, and his reluctance to accept the baby. Plus, Laura would probably advise Kelsie not to go to Pueblo in the middle of the night.

Laura contacted the local law enforcement and told them that her daughter was missing. Without any solid leads or evidence, they started asking around for Kelsie.

Their first step was to take a closer look at Donthe because he claimed that he was the last person to saw Kelsie. She did travel from Denver just to see him. After checking Kelsie's credit card records, they did notice that the card was used hours after Kelsie's last known contact with Donthe. They reviewed the surveillance of the ATM and noticed that Donthe had the card and picked up $400 from Kelsie's account. They weren't sure if Donthe had Kelsie's agreement to use the card, but that was a felony in the state of Colorado, so he was led to the police station for questioning. He had a lot of things to clear up, starting with the timeline of Kelsie's visit to Pueblo.

Donthe's interview

After being picked up by the police, Donthe told his own version of the story. They did see each other that night and talked until early morning hours. Donthe and Kelsie got into a fight and she felt too agitated to drive back home to Denver. She was also very tired from working the second shift. Instead, Kelsie decided to sleep in her car which was parked near his grandmother's house. According to Donthe, his phone rang sometime around 07:00 AM and it was Kelsie. She wasn't feeling well and asked Donthe to drive her to a hospital. He put on his clothes, got to her car, and drove her to the Parkview Hospital.

Kelsie wasn't sure if something happened to the baby during their argument last night and she insisted to see a doctor before she heads out to Denver. Donthe sat inside her car in the parking lot for two hours when she finally emerged from the hospital. Kelsie told him that she had lost the baby. She then asked Donthe to drive her to Walmart to get something to eat and buy some snacks for the road. The two of them started fighting while they were in Walmart and Kelsie refused to drive him home. Donthe simply walked away and got to his grandmother's house on foot. He didn't see Kelsie later in the day and he assumed she went home. He didn't mention stopping at the ATM to pick up the money during his initial interview.

The investigators did notice a couple of possible leads that could collaborate Donthe's story, namely the Parkview Hospital. Each medical facility keeps detailed records of the patients they treat. After speaking to the staff and going through the data, they have confirmed that Kelsie didn't check in during the morning of February 5th. There were also numerous surveillance cameras all over the building and none of them picked up Kelsie entering or leaving the hospital. It was obvious that this part of Donthe's story was not true.

Of course, the police investigators decided to check out Walmart as well because the parking lot and stores do have surveillance cameras, and they might have picked up something that would be of use. While they couldn't find Kelsie or Donthe entering the Walmart, they did notice

Kelsie's car on the parking lot. However, the timeline didn't match up with Donthe's story because Kelsie's car appeared at noon, and not in the morning. Plus, Donthe was the only passenger in the car. Another surveillance camera which was positioned on the back side of Walmart did record Donthe getting into his mother's car – another detail he failed to mention in the initial talk with the investigators.

Without any proof that Donthe's version of the events is true, they called him up for a second interview. The investigators did have a plan this time - they wanted to find out more about the ATM, and how it fits into his timeline. He told the detectives that he took $400 in order to pay his bills and that Kelsie lent him the money since he was at the ATM while Kelsie was at the hospital. When the detectives told Donthe that there is no record of Kelsie ever being in that hospital, his reply was: "I don't even know what to say right now."

They also presented him with Walmart surveillance

video that proves Donthe was the only person in the car. He was surprised with the evidence put in front of him, and before the detectives managed to get him to open up, he decided to lawyer up. He was only charged with the identity theft due to the fact that he used Kelsie's credit card, but the case was dropped. The judge had determined that Donthe did use Kelsie's credit card in the past and it was a normal behavior. However, nobody managed to figure out why Donthe had her card in the first place. After all, if Kelsie decided to ran away and start a new life, she would need the money, as well as her vehicle.

    Speaking of Kelsie's car, the investigators took a closer look at the surveillance video from Walmart parking lot because they wanted to follow the vehicle. Exactly one day after Donthe left Kelsie's car there, another man approached the car and got inside by using the key. He didn't break in or steal the car. The man was dressed in black, wearing a hoodie, so identifying him was almost impossible. His body type was different than Donthe's, and the mystery man was significantly shorter. Keep in mind that Donthe was a tall basketball player, so his height would be noticeable, even in a low-quality video.

Seeing the direction in which the car went, the police collected the surveillance videos from stores and businesses which were in close proximity. They put the puzzle pieces together and found a route but they couldn't follow it all the way. One day later, the car was dropped at the parking lot of Saint Mary Corwin Hospital. The man locked the car and walked away. The investigators located the vehicle on 14th of February, 2013 and figured out the timeline. But nobody knows where the car was during 6th of February. There weren't any signs of a struggle that would indicate that Kelsie was killed in her car. Almost all of her personal items were missing, including her wallet and a backpack.

While it is unclear if the vehicle was tested for the traces of DNA, an unnamed police officer who worked for Pueblo Police Department will later say that they did find bodily fluids in the trunk of Kelsie's car, as well as two palm prints. However, no one knows what happened with this evidence and was it ever tested. It is simply another thing which the police investigators decided to ignore in this case. Unfortunately, the whole investigation will be under scrutiny soon after.

Theories

Figuring out a solid theory without too many evidence or information can be challenging. Laura, Kelsie's mother, claims that her daughter was probably murdered and that it was premeditated. The first red flag for her was Donthe's initial invitation to meet him before the doctor's appointment. When Kelsie refused, he knew that he had to act fast. Donthe lured Kelsie to Pueblo by saying that he has something to show her, but he never gave an explanation to the law enforcement about what the surprise really was.

It is clear that Kelsie was alive and well up until the point she met Donthe in the street next to his grandmother's house. This is where the trail goes cold. The activity on her phone stops until 04:00 AM. If we analyze the location of the phones, another theory is that Donthe led Kelsie to a remote location and harmed her. It was possible that Kelsie dropped her phone in the middle of a struggle. Donthe couldn't find the phone in the dark, so he had to call her number. He was very likely getting rid of the evidence.

There is a possibility that the two of them did indeed get into a fight, and that an unfortunate accident happened. However, it is more likely that Donthe planned to get rid of Kelsie, and had planned every single step he would take that night. He really insisted to see her as soon as possible. While it is not fair to put the blame on the rest of Lucas family, the fact that his mother picked him up immediately after he left Kelsie's vehicle at the Walmart's parking lot indicates that she knew what was going on. Pueblo Police Department did stop investigating Donthe, and they claimed they didn't have enough physical evidence to prove that a crime really occurred. But they did receive a couple of noteworthy tips which were ignored and never pursued.

The missed opportunities

The entire investigation of the disappearance of Kelsie Schelling was troubling from the very beginning. While the detectives did not have physical evidence of a crime, it was clear that Donthe was the last person who saw Kelsie alive. In every standard investigation, he would have been the prime suspect, and the investigators would do their best to find more proof that he was somehow connected to the crime. The cell tower pings did show that both of their phones were in a remote area next to Pueblo in the early morning hours.

But there are even bigger missed opportunities that could have provided the investigators with the proof they needed. For instance, Donthe was living in his grandmother's house at the time of Kelsie's disappearance. However, the entire family moved out soon after. The landlord started redecorating the house because he wanted to rent it again. He did hear about the missing girl from Denver but had no idea about the details of the case, or the fact that the Lucas family was involved in any way.

He decided to put the new carpets in and when he lifted the old one, the landlord noticed a strange stain on the bottom. He contacted the police enforcement because he was worried that something bad has happened in the house. However, the police ignored his request to check out the stained carpet, and no one had ever arrived at Lucas' previous residence to pick it up. The landlord ended up throwing the carpet away because he simply couldn't keep it forever in the house and wanted to move on with the renovation.

Another missed opportunity involved a couple of fishermen who were out on a lake on a night fishing expedition. It is important to mention that the lake was located near the Saint Mary Corwin Hospital. As you might recall, that was the spot where the police officers discovered Kelsie's vehicle on the 14th of February 2013.

They were out on a bank when a hook got stuck to something poking out of the sand. The fishermen went to investigate and were sure that they saw a part of a human ribcage, as well as a skull.

They were terrified by that discovery and left the area right away. Both of them were reluctant to notify the police because they did have some troubles with the law in the past. But that didn't stop them from telling this story to their friends who urged them to contact the local law enforcement. A couple of months passed before they finally talked to the police, but the lake wasn't searched afterward.

The current searches

Family and friends continued to search for Kelsie even after it was clear that the police enforcement forgot about her case. They created a Facebook group that was constantly updated with new information. Pueblo Police Department did go through many changes after Kelsie went missing. The lead investigator was replaced with a new one who was willing to cooperate with the Schelling family. The Schellings did offer a large reward for any new leads that might help them locate their missing daughter. The reward was $100,000 at one point.

This eventually led to false claims and misleading messages such as the one which claimed that Kelsie was still alive, but was placed into a sex traffic ring after a hired hitman decided not to kill her. Laura Schelling contacted the police and told them about the message. Since the investigators decided to follow every lead possible, they dug deeper and even involved the FBI. Their experts did manage to trace the message back to Russia through the IP address so it was clear that this tip was useless.

The biggest break in the case happened in the spring of 2017 when Colorado Bureau of Investigation finally got the authorization from the local law enforcement to join the search. CBI did determine that the prime suspect should be Donthe Lucas, and they got the warrant to search the area around his previous place of residence. A large number of police officers was seen around that house during April of 2017, and they dug up the parts of the backyard using heavy machinery.

The search has been successful and the officers left the scene carrying bags of evidence. However, they stated that they didn't find any traces of Kelsie's remains. Kelsie's family released the following statement after the search: "The past 2 days have been grueling and emotional, ending with the outcome we did not hope for. Kelsie is still missing. There is no way for me to convey to you all the pain that I feel right now. Sincere, heartfelt thanks goes out to the members of Pueblo PD, CBI and Parks & Rec who worked so hard on this search for Kelsie. This was a physically demanding excavation for them and we witnessed how hard they worked. Despite all the issues we have had in the past, the new leadership over Kelsie's case from PPD and active involvement from CBI is giving us hope that an effective investigation is finally taking place."

The case is still active and the police didn't arrest Donthe. But the positive changes are happening and Kelsie's family is certain that they will find the answers they are looking for now that the investigation is finally moving forward.

FOREVER MISS-ING: THE DIS-APPEARANCE OF NATALEE HOLLOWAY

NATHAN NIXON

Natalee Holloway Disappearance

The tragic story of Natalee Holloway still remains a mystery to this day. The events prior to her disappearance are centered on unreliable witnesses, investigators not following proper procedures, and friends who had left her alone with local patrons. To say that a school trip is never supposed to turn out this way is a monumental understatement. Several theories exist as to what really happened to Natalee. The one, glaring truth of the matter is that Natalee was a beautiful, vibrant young woman who is gone far too soon. Many other facts exist. Witnesses, however, do not.

Natalee Holloway was born in 1986 to David and

Elizabeth Holloway in Clinton, Mississippi. Following her parents mutual divorce in 1993, she was raised by her mother alongside her younger brother. Natalee made her life in Alabama when her mother re-married to George Twitty. It was here that she prospered in many organizations, extracurricular activities, and academic niches. Natalee attended Mountain Brook High School in Mountain Brook, Alabama. She was a prominent member in the National Honor Society, was a leader on the school dance team, and competed several sports. Through her hard work, she had earned a full scholarship to attend the University of Alabama, where she enter a pre-med course track and eventually earn her Doctorate. This was all assuming she would make it to the next fall.

Upon graduation, 124 graduating Mountain Brook High School seniors took an "unofficial" school trip to Aruba. Aruba is a Dutch holding in the Caribbean. The group of students arrived in Aruba on May 26, 2005. The trip was scheduled for five days. Oddities of this trip were already apparent. While the trip had 7 chaperones, the students were not expected to be watched every second. The chaperones would meet with the full group of students each night to make sure that everything was okay. To say that these students were taking advantage of this was an understatement. "There was wild partying, lots of drinking, lots of room switching every night," Police Commissioner Gerold Dompig, who headed the investigation from mid-2005 to late 2016, said. "We are aware that the Holiday Inn told them they were absolutely not welcome back next year. Natalee, we know, drank all day every day while there. We have statements that proclaim she started every morning with cocktails. Often times so much drinking that she didn't show up for breakfast on two separate mornings."

Liz Cain and Claire Foreman, two of Holloway's classmates, agreed. "The drinking was excessive. We all were going too far and didn't understand the dangers"

Jodi Bearman organized the class trip. The investigation that would soon follow turned up numerous mistakes and irresponsibility's on the part of organizers and chaperones. The obvious problem was the supervision. How can seven chaperones have control of 124 high school graduates in a foreign place? These students were essentially given the freedom to do whatever they wanted with no punishment. Investigators and parents alike could not believe the lack of supervision and authority displayed by the adults. The punishment that Natalee Holloway would suffer was far greater than anyone could have imagined. However, the fact that this was an avoidable mistake is obvious. Natalee Holloway should never have been allowed to be in this position.

It was May 29, 2005. Natalee had packed her luggage and prepared all of her things to board the flight home the next morning. She had positioned her luggage neatly at the foot of her bed and cleaned up her hotel room accordingly. The 124 graduates had one last night of fun before it was time to head home. This was the last time she would be in her hotel room.

Natalee went out on the town with several of her classmates on night of May 29. Typical of the previous nights, she and her classmates had been heavily drinking and interacting with numerous locals. Natalee had a contagious personality and could always strike up a conversation with anyone. As the night drew on into morning, they arrived at Carlos'n Charlies. This was a well-known bar and dance club in the heart of Aruba. Natalee would last be seen at approximately 1:30 A.M. on May 30, 2005. The story was only just beginning.

Natalee had met up with locals seemingly every night she went out. Striking up conversations, drinking excessively, and trusting strangers was common by several of the graduates that were there. The last glimpse of Natalee would prove to be the beginning of a complicated, international investigation that would prove nearly impossible to solve. She left the club that morning with 17-year-old Joran van der Sloot, 21-year-old Deepak Kalpoe, and 18-year-old Satish Kalpoe. The events that took place after that are largely contested. Through many different testimonies by witnesses and suspects, investigators would check every lead and run into heartbreaking dead ends.

Upon the morning sunrise, the graduates arrived to board the flight home. It was time to start the rest of their lives. All of the graduates arrived without problem except for one: Natalee Holloway. Through irresponsible chaperoning of a class trip and complete disregard for holding the safety of these students paramount above a fun time, an 18-year-old girl was missing. Her hotel room looked untouched from the previous evening. Her luggage safely packed in anticipation of leaving. No signs of movement in the room. Not even a towel had been disturbed. It was frighteningly clear that she had not returned to her room from the previous night's adventures. When the students and chaperones realized what was going on, they immediately notified authorities. Aruban police initiated immediate searches of the island and its surrounding waters. No trace of her was found.

Joran van der Sloot is undoubtedly the most central figure to this case. Van der Sloot was a 17-year-old Dutch honors student who lived in Aruba. At first glance, his baby face and focused eyes would seemingly make him very approachable to anyone. This was, apparently, not the first night that Natalee and Joran had met. In previous nights, they hung out at bars and engaged in behavior not known to most high school students. Over the course of the next several years, Joran would lead investigators and the Holloway family on a wild goose chase that involved changing alibis, secret videos, and fraud. The innocent appearance that Joran van der Sloot displayed was only a disguise for the true monster he would prove to be.

The Kalpoe brothers were Surinamese friends of

van der Sloot. Their significance is much less publicized beyond the last sighting of Holloway. Natalee was last seen getting into Deepak Kalpoe's car with both van der Sloot and Satish. This has been confirmed true by both witnesses and suspects in one way or another. There are numerous stories told by van Sloot and other later suspects that bring the Kalpoe's back to the forefront of the case. In such a complicated investigation, Joran van der Sloot, Deepak Kalpoe, and Satish Kalpoe emerged as early suspects.

Action was fast when news reached family of the mysterious disappearance of Natalee. Her mother, Beth Twitty, immediately boarded a private jet with friends and departed for Aruba. Upon arriving in Aruba, the Twittys had started searching for themselves. They located the Holiday Inn and began asking questions. They had obtained footage from the nightclub she was last seen at. To Beth Twittys surprise, the Holiday Inn workers recognized Joran van der Sloot instantly. He had apparently been a regular in the area. The helpful Holiday Inn employees provided Beth and company with Joran's name and address. Within a mere four hours since arriving at Aruba, the Twittys had already obtained more information than investigators had been able to. The Twittys provided Aruba Police with this information. It appeared that a case was forming around Van der Sloot already. However, the mishandling of the case and poor techniques of the Aruba Police Department were already rearing their ugly head. This case would prove to be a showcase of poor work, bitter disappointment, and investigators being led around by the suspects themselves. The first lead, however, was officially created.

The Twittys and their friends went to the home of Joran van der Sloot. They were accompanied by two Aruban policemen. The fact that Van der Sloot was even allowed to be approached in this manner showed quickly the lack of thought given to the early stages of the investigation. At this early point in the case, the extent of the crime was largely unknown. Hoping for the best, the Twittys only wished to find Natalee safely at the home of Van der Sloot. Joran answered the door and initially denied even knowing who Natalee Holloway was. After being confronted with evidence of their rendezvous that morning, Van der Sloot admitted to being with Natalee. Also present at the house was Deepak Kalpoe, who was driving the vehicle that Natalee had entered in to.

Van der Sloot gave a sketchy story of what had happened after they left the nightclub. He informed the Twittys as well as the two policemen that they had taken Natalee to the California Lighthouse area. This area was near the nightclub, perhaps a few miles drive depending on the route taken. Natalee had been emphatic that she wanted to see sharks. After leaving the nightclub at 1:30 A.M. they went straight to this area to sight see. Van der Sloot informed them that they had returned Natalee to the Holiday Inn hotel where she had been staying at 2:00 A.M. Natalee, who was heavily intoxicated, stumbled exiting the vehicle. The men had offered to help Natalee to her room, however she refused their help and continued toward the entrance. It was at this time, according to Van der Sloot, that she was approached by a tall man wearing all black. Thinking this was a security guard, the men drove off. This, according to Van der Sloot, was the last interaction of any kind with Natalee Holloway that they had. Deepak Kalpoe affirmed the story and agreed with the events.

This is the initial story of the events. The initial investigation is, perhaps, the most ridiculed part in this case. Not only were the men not detained for further extensive questioning, they were completely presumed to be telling the truth. This not only wasted valuable time in finding Natalee, it also allowed suspects to plan their next move. The fact that Van der Sloot and Kalpoe had initially denied even knowing who Natalee Holloway was should have been the first sign of a problem. The second, and more major sign of a problem would come in the investigation of the hotel surveillance footage. While this was obviously looked at during the investigation, this is largely an accepted procedure that is typically done prior to confronting a potential suspect.

The surveillance footage, or lack thereof, was arguably the single biggest setback with this case. The fact that Natalee was not seen in any hotel footage that fateful morning would lend investigators to believe that Van der Sloot and Kalpoe were lying. The hitch in this was that many statements from the case could not even prove that all cameras were functional at the time. The next problem was the fact that not every entrance had a surveillance. This would leave reasonable doubt that Natalee could have been dropped off near one of these entrances that was simply inaccessible to the surveillance footage.

Investigators finally felt as though they had caught the break in the case they needed when a blood stain was found in Deepak Kalpoe's car. Searching the car that was captured on surveillance as the same one that transported Natalee Holloway from the nightclub, police discovered what appeared to be a blood stain. After lab testing and further investigation, not only was this not Natalee Holloway's blood, it could not even be proven to be blood at all. Another door was closed in the initial investigation of Natalee's disappearance.

After the first full day of investigation, United States involvement in the case began. Monetary assistance was given immediately to aid the Aruban Police Department. Additionally, American searchers sought to help with the advanced search of coastline that had been a constant since Natalee Holloway missed her flight. United States Secretary of State Condoleezza Rice stated "we are in constant contact with Aruban Police. The safe return of Natalee Holloway continues to be our priority."

Hours after missing her flight, the media's involvement in the case was tremendous. All of the major news stations in the United States began their initial coverage of the story. With little facts to go on, it was largely reported as a missing person case with no evidence of foul play. No suspects had truly been pinpointed at this point. The news of her last being seen in the early hours leaving a nightclub led several to assume the worst from the get go, however. It would not be long before Joran van der Sloot was at the fore front of the investigation as well as the ensuing media storm.

It was just six days after Holloway's disappearance that authorities made their first arrest in the case. On June 5, 2005, Abraham Jones and Nick John were placed under arrest. To this day, the exact reasoning behind their arrest is unknown. One of the men had previous encounters with the law, while both were suspected of previously pacing hotels to pick up women. Both men were security guards at a nearby hotel, the Allegro Hotel. It is likely that the statements made by Van der Sloot and Kalpoe led police to this arrest. The men were released on June 13 with no charges being placed. This is yet another example of flawed work by the investigation. It was obvious that police were trusting of Joran van der Sloot and Deepak Kalpoe from the onset. This is a largely debated topic to this day. Many wonder why Van der Sloot and Kalpoe were not arrested initially. However, this was just scratching the surface of what was to come.

On June 9, Joran van der Sloot and both Kalpoe brothers were arrested on suspicion of the kidnapping and murder of Natalee Holloway. In hindsight, it is absolutely unfathomable that it took investigators 10 days to make these arrest. The only evidence they really had at this point was surveillance of Natalee last being seen with these men. Aruban police reported that these men were the "prime suspects from the get-go." While this may have been true to a point, police waited until June 6 to start extended surveillance of the men. Investigators knew they would need much more evidence than a video of Natalee entering a car with the men from the nightclub. Aruban Police instigated phone taps, video surveillance, tailing their vehicles, and monitoring of their e-mails. At this point, in order to continue to hold the three suspects in custody, they would need to provide increasingly substantial evidence at different check points of the investigation. With increasingly consistent pressure from Natalee Holloway's family, police decided to stop the surveillance activities prematurely and execute the arrest on the men.

The arrest of these three suspects was met with heavy interest from people all over the world. The procedures by police and the heavy involvement of the Holloway family seemingly left everyone with an opinion on what should have been conducted differently. Many media outlets focused on the timing of the surveillance activities. Having taken nearly a week to begin the activities from the time of Natalee's last sighting, many felt it was already too late to incriminate the suspects. Also, the fact that surveillance started at the time they had already arrested Adams and

John was a bit odd for normal investigative procedure. Lastly, many assumed that if investigators pursued an arrest after just a few days of surveillance of the men, they must have captured something indisputable to implicate one or all of the suspects. This was simply not the case. Aruban Police had missed the initial window of the investigation. Many critics argue that in the interest of uncovering the truth, an extended surveillance would be necessary for the time period they had waited to begin. Investigators instead buckled to pressure from an unorthodox family interaction in a complicated case.

June 11 was the first of many highly publicized false leads. Aruban Minister of Justice David Cruz indicated, in a statement, that Natalee Holloway was dead and that authorities knew the exact location of her body. This was all over most any major media outlet as an early morning breaking news story. The United States was gripped with curiosity and heartbreak as it seemed the terrible truth had come to fruition. Hours later, Cruz released a follow up statement that they had been the victim of "misinformation." This simply is unacceptable. As an investigator or someone in a position as high as Cruz was, you can't put the wagon before the horse, especially to national media outlets. What was the source of this misinformation? Lead investigator Gerold Dompig reported to the Associated Press that one of the detained men had informed them that "something terrible and unthinkable" had happened on the beach after they left the nightclub. The suspect, it was reported, was leading them to the location of the body. This, of course, was another folly.

On June 16, yet another suspect, Steve Gregory Croes, was arrested. "Croes was detained based on urgent information given to us by one of the other three suspect," Aruban Police Superintendent Jan van der Straaten informed the media. While this arrest didn't yield much as far as new leads, it did start to give the appearance that investigators were at a standstill with the case. Six days later on June 22, Joran van der Sloot's father, Paulus, was arrested. This was largely believed to be a bargaining chip to use against Joran. While Paulus was not a suspect, as later revealed by police, he was interrogated in an effort to get more information on Joran. Both Croes and Paulus van der

Sloot were released on June 26.

It was around this time where public opinion began to focus on Joran van der Sloot. It was quite clear to all involved that Van der Sloot was not being truthful in his story. The events made little sense to the general public. The longer that Natalee remained missing, the more likely it was that she was, indeed, dead. The suspicion on Joran would only intensify in the coming day.

From the time of the arrest of Joran van der Sloot and the Kalpoe brothers, their stories changed numerous times. In particular, Van der Sloot was giving three completely conflicting stories that would put the focus solely on him.

The first story shift came, oddly enough, from all three suspects. Van der Sloot and both Kalpoe brothers all agreed that Joran and Natalee had been dropped off at the Marriott Hotel beach near several fisherman huts. Van der Sloot was emphatic that he didn't harm Natalee Holloway in any way. He told investigators that they were both heavily intoxicated, and eventually Natalee passed out on the beach. When this happened, he began to walk home. It was at this time that he made a phone call to Deepak Kalpoe that he was walking home. Van der Sloot claims to have sent Kalpoe a text message 40 minutes later. Oddly enough, the phone call nor text message was found in Van der Sloot's phone records.

Lead investigator Gerold Dompig gave insight into the third different story by the suspects. This story, told by Joran van der Sloot, was a turning point in that it showed that he was willing to change his story however he saw fit in order to avoid suspicion.

"The latest story came when Joran saw that his buddies, the Kalpoe's, were essentially pointing the finger in his direction. He wanted to screw them by pointing the finger right back at them. But the story simply doesn't check out. He just wanted to screw Deepak. They (Deepak and Joran) had great arguments about this in front of the judge. Their stories didn't match. Joran felt the focus shifting to him and was willing to do anything to change it. That girl, she was from Alabama. She is not going to stay in the car with two black kids while Joran simply gets out of the car to head home alone. We firmly believe the second story;

that they were dropped off at the Marriott. This goes along with the timeline and the stories given by the Kalpoe's."

Upon hearings in front of the judge on July 4, both Satish and Deepak Kalpoe were released from custody. Joran van der Sloot was to remain for a minimum of 60 days. Focus was solely on Van der Sloot as the main suspect in the disappearance of Natalee Holloway.

For nearly all of July, searches for Natalee Holloway remained fruitless endeavors. Investigators had no leads and were consistently getting varied stories from Joran van der Sloot. While police had solid suspicions of Van der Sloot, they had essentially zero solid evidence against him. The media storm updated the world daily on search efforts. With each passing day, reality began to set in for many that Natalee Holloway may never be found. Initially, a $50,000 reward was offered for Natalee's safe return. On July 25, the reward for the safe return of Holloway had increased all the way to $1,000,000. In addition, a $100,000 reward was offered for information that would lead to the location of her remains. In August of the same year, the reward for the location of her remains would raise all the way to $250,000. This was widely covered by the media and many local and national governments. This was a final attempt by investigators to break the cold case open. This strategy had several negative impacts, however. The most severe of these were the wasted time on false leads and folly calls. This was not anticipated by investigators as it should have been.

Between July 27 and 30, investigators initiated a massive undertaking. The pond in front of the Aruba Racquet Club was completely drained. This was within one mile of the Marriott Hotel where Van der Sloot had apparently taken Natalee Holloway. A tip was given to police that was especially unique. A gardener had apparently seen Joran van der Sloot driving into the Racquet Club with the Kalpoe brothers. Van der Sloot was said to have been hiding his face. The gardener informed police that the men were seen driving in between 2:30 A.M. and 3:00 A.M. on the morning of May 30. The search of the pond bed and surrounding area, however, yielded no clues.

On July 28, a jogger came forward with a frightening testimony. The United States media covered this story heavily for several days as it was the first story of someone seeing a woman resembling Natalee Holloway since her disappearance. The jogger claimed that she saw a group of men burying a young, blonde haired woman on the afternoon of May 30 at a landfill. The landfill was subsequently searched three separate times with precision. This search, again, yielded no results.

In late August, Joran van der Sloot became the front page villain to many. Throughout the entire case, it was well covered as to how many variations of a story Joran had given. While showing no remorse or empathy for the Holloway family, the public formed a very negative opinion of Van der Sloot. Anita van der Sloot would provide more material for the family. "It's a desperate attempt to get the boys to talk. But there is nothing to talk about. Joran has no fault in this mystery." Joran van der Sloot's mother made this statement after police again brought in the Kalpoe's for questioning. This left a bitter taste in the mouths of many. It was shaping up to be Van der Sloot's versus investigators.

On September 3, 2005, Joran van der Sloot was released from custody due to insufficient evidence to hold. By September 14, all restrictions were officially lifted from Van der Sloot. Whatever the events of May 30, no suspect was in custody and there were no leads for police. Joran van der Sloot was a free man. The release of Van der Sloot created a frenzy among the general public. People all over the United States and surrounding areas were furious, set in their beliefs that a guilty man was walking away free. The nation was gripped against a common villain.

The months that followed Joran van der Sloot's release provided media cannon fodder of epic proportions. Van der Sloot did several interviews and even composed a book of his take on the events of the night. To the public's astonishment, this man was now profiting off of this whole fire storm of a case. The most notable post release interview came with Fox News on a three night special. Van der Sloot claims that the two were heavily intoxicated on the beach after leaving the nightclub. He went into great detail about the two planning an escapade on the beach, narcotic use, and partying in a fun filled night in Aruba. He showed little empathy or remorse for any of the events. He seemingly talked about Natalee as if she was the villain. Joran went on to explain that Natalee wanted to have sex on the beach, however he didn't have a condom. He left her on the beach and was driven home by Satish Kalpoe. Later, Satish Kalpoe's lawyer claims that Satish was asleep well before this would have happened. Joran went on to explain that he was embarrassed for having left a beautiful woman alone on the beach, citing this as the reason for his ever changing story. He said that he was convinced Holloway would turn up.

This all sat so negatively to viewers. There was

outrage over the handling of the investigation. People could not understand how no evidence existed to implicate a man that was deemed the perpetrator. Aruba authorities later claimed that over $3 million had been spent on the investigation. This was over 40% of the overall budget for investigative expenditures.

On December 18, 2007 after extensive efforts to implicate the Kalpoe brothers and/or Joran van der Sloot, the case was officially closed. Prosecutors cited lack of evidence to a violent crime, lack of evidence to a murder, as well as lack of continued funding for the expensive investigation. Over two full years after the disappearance of Natalee Holloway, the case was closed. The remains of Natalee Holloway had not been found. Joran van der Sloot not only was a free man, but had profited greatly from the publicity of the case. This, however, would not be the final chapter to the journey of Joran van der Sloot.

In the years after the closing of the Natalee Holloway case, Joran van der Sloot told several variations of events of that fateful morning. He gave countless interviews, seemingly telling a different story in each one of them. Ultimately, Joran van der Sloot was seeking money and fame through his disgusting actions. In an interview with Fox News in 2008, he claimed to have sold Natalee Holloway in sexual slavery. He later retracted the statements in the days after. It was reported in 2010 that in a 2009 interview with RTL group, he claimed he disposed of the body in a marsh area in Aruba. This interview was never confirmed, nor denied by investigators or Van der Sloot.

Remarkably, Van der Sloot would show his greed had no limits. On March 29, 2010 Van der Sloot contacted Beth Twittys legal representative. He offered to give the location to Natalee Holloway's remains in exchange for $25,000. After contacting police, the transaction was made. $15,000 was wired to Van der Sloot's account, and the remaining $10,000 was given by a middle man. The receipt of the transaction was videotaped by police. The information provided by Van der Sloot was proven false, as the building that he claimed housed the remains was not yet built at the time of the disappearance. Van der Sloot would be indicted on June 30 of the same year. However, he was about to be indicted for a much more serious crime.

On May 30, 2010, exactly five years from the time of the disappearance of Natalee Holloway, Stephany Flores Ramirez was reported missing in Lima, Peru. Ironically, she was found dead just three days later in a hotel room registered to Joran van der Sloot. On June 7, 2010, Van der Sloot confessed to killing Ramirez after he lost his temper while she was using his laptop. Within the same interview, he said that he knew where Holloway's body was. Dealing with jurisdiction issues, Peruvian police could not further investigate the Holloway statement without Aruban authorities.

Aruban authorities were granted interrogation of Van der Sloot in Peru in June of 2010. While he would not confess to murdering Holloway or her whereabouts, he did admit to the extortion plot on the Holloway family. "I wanted to get back at Natalee's family. They have been making my life miserable for the last five years," Van der Sloot said. Van der Sloot was found guilty in the murder of Stephany Flores Ramirez and sentenced to 28 years in prison. This sentence also included his time for his extortion of the Holloway family.

    Natalee Holloway's remains have never been found. There have never been any convictions made into the disappearance of Natalee or any criminal wrong doing. In this case, it would be naïve to imagine a scenario where Joran van der Sloot was not responsible in some way for the death of Natalee Holloway. While Van der Sloot waste the best years of his life behind bars, a young woman with an extremely bright future is still gone. Closure will never be possible for the Holloway family. Perhaps a poor investigative strategy is to blame for the lack of any convictions. Maybe it is the irresponsible planning of school personnel and behavior supervision by chaperones could have prevented this tragedy. Better decision by Natalee herself may have helped avoid such a terrible event. In any case, an intelligent young woman who had everything in front of her did not deserve this end. The Holloway family did not deserve this. We will likely never know the true events of that fateful May morning. What we do know is that we will never get to see the true potential that Natalee Holloway had.

FINDING JENNIFER : THE DISAPPEARANCE OF JENNIFER KESSE

MARY DANIELLE TAYLOR

The unsolved disappearance of Jennifer Kesse from her

Orlando, Florida condo in the early hours of January 23, 2006, garnered widespread attention from the local and national media alike, leading to large-scale search parties conducted by the Orlando Police Department and FBI. However, despite the fact that Jennifer Kesse disappeared over ten years ago in the parking lot of her apartment complex, investigators are no closer to solving the case.

Jennifer Kesse, a finance manager for a Florida property and vacation company, had left her recently purchased condo in Orlando, Florida to begin her morning commute to work. However, Jennifer would never make it into work that morning, and her family and friends would never hear from her again. Read on to learn more about who Jennifer Kesse was, about the circumstances of her disappearance, and the local and national reaction to her missing persons case.

Early Life

Jennifer Kesse, a graduate of Vivian Gaither High School in Tampa, Florida, had graduated with a degree in finance from the University of Central Florida, located in Orlando, Florida, in 2003, where she also served as a member of the Alpha Delta Pi sorority. Following her graduation from college, Jennifer began working at the Central Florida Investments Timeshare Company as a finance manager.

Shortly before the date of her disappearance, Jennifer and her current boyfriend had visited Saint Croix, in the U.S. Virgin Islands, for a vacation. After returning home from the Virgin Islands by plane, Jennifer drove directly from her boyfriend's house in South Florida to her job in Ocoee, Florida for a full day of work. Jennifer would return home to her newly-purchased condo in Orlando that evening, the very same evening of her disappearance.

Night of Her Disappearance

Jennifer was last seen leaving the Westgate Resorts office of the Central Florida Investments Timeshare Company on the night of January 23, 2006 in Ocoee, Florida, after returning home from her vacation in Saint Croix, in the U.S. Virgin Islands, with her boyfriend. Several close friends and members of her family received calls from Jennifer that night, and the last call that she made before her disappearance was to her boyfriend shortly before 10:00pm.

Jennifer typically called or texted her boyfriend during her morning commute to work to wish him good morning; however, he became concerned on the morning of January 24th when he did not receive a message from her. When he attempted to call Jennifer that morning, his call was sent directly to voicemail. Because Jennifer had previously told him that she had an early-morning meeting at work, he assumed that she was busy and would call him once she received his voicemail. He continued his day at work until receiving a call from Jennifer's parents later that day informing him that she had never made it to work.

When Jennifer did not show up to work or contact her direct supervisor, a coworker contacted Jennifer's parents to express concern and see if they had heard from her. Jennifer was supposed to attend a very important work meeting with her higher-ups that morning, and it was extremely unlike her to fail to show up with calling ahead. Upon receiving the call from Jennifer's office, her parents immediately jumped into action. Her father, Drew Kesse, said "We were calling hospitals, calling jails, calling her friends, asking them to call places, calling Rob, and he tried calling her and she did not answer."

Her parents soon jumped into their car and made the two-hour drive to Jennifer's condo in Orlando, Florida from their home in Tampa. While driving, her parents contact her condo management office at *Mosaic Apartments*, located on the 3700 block Convoy Road in Orlando, and requested that the manager stop by her condo to check on her. He reported that she was not home, that her condo was in great condition, and that her car was not in the parking lot.

In addition, once her parents arrived in Orlando and entered their daughter's condo, they did not notice anything out of place or any signs of a struggle. Furthermore, they noticed that Jennifer's clothes were laid out on her bed and that a wet towel was present in the restroom, leading them to believe that Jennifer was at home that morning. Her father Drew later said, "We actually found two or three outfits laid out on her bed she was picking. Showered, shower was still damp. Her towel was still damp. Her work stuff was not there. So we knew that, OK, she got ready for work."

The parents quickly contacted the Orlando police department to report her as missing. Family members began passing out flyers that evening and reaching out to local media organizations, while the local police department began organizing a search party.

A local television reporter and friend of Jennifer's, Scott Thuman, described the family's actions like this: "I made sure they were on every TV station every single night as long as we could keep that alive. They did the networks, they did radio shows. They did every newspaper interview they could." An investigative reporter who covered the case would later say, "It was hard to go anywhere without seeing her face and her picture and also the information on her vehicle."

Timeline

January 23, 2006

Early Morning – Leaves her boyfriend's home in Central Florida to head directly to her office at Westgate Resorts for a full day at work. Jennifer and her boyfriend had just returned from a trip to Saint Croix, U.S. Virgin Islands.

6:00pm – Jennifer leaves her office at Westgate Resorts and drives to her condo complex in Orlando, Florida. She unpacks her clothes and contacts several family members to let them know that she has returned home from vacation safely.

10:00pm – Jennifer calls her boyfriend and speaks with him for several minutes before saying goodnight. Jennifer's boyfriend is the last known person to speak with her before her disappearance.

January 24, 2006

7:30am – Police believe that Jennifer was abducted sometime around 7:30am to 8:00am on the morning of the 24th. She was likely taken either while walking through the parking lot towards her car or while entering her vehicle.

8:30am – Jennifer's boyfriend calls her, but the call is sent directly to voicemail. Jennifer typically calls her boyfriend during her morning commute to say good morning and chat. He assumes that she is busy with an early-morning meeting that they had previously discussed.

11:00am – Jennifer's coworkers, concerned that she uncharacteristically did not show up to work and had missed a very important meeting, called her parents to see if Jennifer is okay. Both her parents and coworkers realize that something is wrong.

11:15am – Jennifer's parents immediately begin the two-hour drive to Jennifer's condo in Orlando from their home in Tampa. Her parents contact her condo's management office and request that they enter her condo to check on her. He reports that nothing is out of the ordinary and that her car is gone.

12:00pm – Jennifer's brother, who lives locally, arrives at her condo complex and begins looking for her. Unbeknownst to anyone at the time, a surveillance camera at an apartment complex 1 mile down the road from her own condo shows an unidentifiable man parking Jennifer's car. The video shows the suspect parking the car, and sitting in it for approximately 30 seconds before exiting the car and walking away from the complex. Unfortunately for investigators, the suspect's face was obscured by a fencing post and neither the local police department nor the FBI were able to produce a useable shot of the suspect's face.

1:00pm – Jennifer's parents arrive in Orlando and immediately enter her condo. They notice that her shower is covered with water and that her towel is still wet. They also see that her work clothes are laid out on her unmade bed, that her makeup and hairdryer are lying out on her bathroom sink, and that her pajamas are piled on the restroom floor. Police theorize that Jennifer may have had a fight with her boyfriend and left her apartment to cool off.

They preach patience to the parents.

5:00pm – Jennifer's close family and friends begin passing out missing persons flyers to local passerby. The police respond by sending a detective to her condo to gather information and investigate her disappearance. Police begin to question her family and friends, and begin to organize a search party.

January 26, 2006

8:10am – After seeing a report on Jennifer's disappearance on the local news, a resident at a local apartment complex calls the Orlando Police Department to report that her car has been parked in their complex for the last two days. Police arrive at the complex to verify this report, and quickly haul the car away to local police facilities for a forensic analysis. Police are finally able to identify and locate security footage showing an unidentified person parking Jennifer's car and leaving the complex by foot. This footage would lead investigators to determine that Jennifer may have been abducted.

Investigation

Jennifer's parents, as well as the initial investigators who looked into her case, noticed that Jennifer's apartment showed no signs of forced entry, her condo door was locked, and there were no signs of a struggle. Furthermore, because Jennifer's work clothes were laid out neatly and there was evidence that she had recently showered, investigators theorized that she had gotten ready for work the morning of her disappearance and had left her condo to begin her morning commute. The also assert that Jennifer likely left her apartment and was abducted either during the walk to her car or as she was entering the vehicle.

Two days after Jennifer's disappearance on January 26th, her 2004 black Chevy Malibu was located at the *Huntington on the Green* apartment complex, located at Americana Ave. and Texas, a little over a mile away from her own condo. While the apartment complex her car was parked at did have several security cameras, covering both her car and the exit to the apartment complex itself, the videos offered limited clues to her disappearance.

The video showed a "person of interest" who dropped off her car at noon the day of her disappearance; however, the best shots from the video were rendered useless since fencing from the apartment complex concealed the face of the unidentified man in three separate frames. The suspect was seen wearing an all-white uniform, leading some close to the case to believe that the suspect was a painter or other type of manual laborer.

Beau Zimmer, an investigative reporter who followed Jennifer Kesse's disappearance, described the video like this: "There's two different angles, all surrounding the pool area. But it's very, very blurry and it's hard to see. But you can see someone pulling Jennifer's car into that visitor's parking lot. They wait inside the car for a number of seconds before they get out and look around, and then walk out of frame of the picture. But the next shot of the video was what everyone thought would be so helpful. The next shot was of a person that was walking back and forth along the fence line."

However, he noted, "Every frame of the video, the person is obscured by a post and so you never see the person's face." Zimmer would later remark, "It has got to be the most frustrating thing for detectives, the most frustrating thing for the Kesse family, because for just one split second, later or earlier, you would have seen that individual's face and you would have had a better idea of what happened to Jennifer."

When investigators shared footage from the video with Jennifer's family and friends, they were unable to identify the man in question. A Fox News reporter would later say in a televised retrospective segment on the case that the obscured image made the man the "luckiest person of interest ever."

Both the FBI and NASA were called in to conduct advanced video analyses of the footage to provide more clues on the stalled case. The FBI determined that the person was roughly 5'3" to 5'5" tall, but could not offer definitive proof of the suspect's gender. Despite NASA's digital enhancement of the video, they were not able to provide any additional information that could help the case.

Despite the dead-end that the surveillance video represented, investigators were able to put together several pieces of the puzzle. Since all of Jennifer's valuables were found in her car, parked a mile down the street in a different apartment complex, they were able to determine that robbery was not a primary motive in her disappearance. In addition, a police dog was able to track a scent a full mile from her parked car back to her condo complex, leading investigators to theorize that the unidentified suspect returned to her complex directly after disposing of her car. However, police were unable to locate any helpful evidence along the route walked by the suspect.

After conducted a search and forensic analysis of her

vehicle, investigators identified two pieces of evidence: a latent fingerprint from an unidentified individual and a small strand of DNA. Given the lack of evidence found in the car, coupled with the lack of clothing fibers, hair strands, and DNA, the police believe that the car was thoroughly wiped down in an attempt to remove incriminating evidence. The investigative reporter assigned to the case, Beau Zimmer, would say, "There was maybe one print and detectives think that it was maybe wiped down, and that this was an intentional act to not only hide this vehicle, but also to hide any evidence of who may have driven it."

Despite the lack of evidence found in her car, investigators did notice that several items were missing. They were unable to located her cell phone, keys, purse, clothes, briefcase, or iPod. While police are often able to track a missing person's cell phone or bank accounts for clues, her bank account was never accessed by her captors and her cell phone remained turned off with the battery removed.

Investigators quickly compiled a list of potential suspects after questioning her friends and family for clues. Her current boyfriend was questioned and quickly eliminated from the list of suspects after providing a valid alibi. In addition, Jennifer's ex-boyfriend and one of her coworkers, who had romantic feelings for Jennifer and had sought a relationship with her in the past, were interviewed by the police.

One the of the most interesting factors in Jennifer's disappearance was the fact that her condo complex was undergoing major construction at the time of her disappearance. Many of the workers, some who were undocumented immigrants, were living in the complex while it was undergoing construction. Jennifer had mentioned her discomfort with some of the workers to her family on multiple occasions, claiming that they harassed and catcalled her regularly. Jennifer's parents have also stated on multiple occasions that they believe she may have been a victim of human trafficking.

In May 2007, the CEO of Central Florida Investments Timeshare Company, David Siegel, offered a $1 million reward for information that led to her being found alive; however, the reward was never claimed. A $5,000 reward for information on her disappearance, offered by the Central Florida Crime line, remains active today.

Suspects

Ex-boyfriend

Jennifer had recently broken up with a previous boyfriend, and he was reportedly very angry about the breakup and the fact that Jennifer was now dating another man. Beau Zimmer would report that Jennifer's ex-boyfriend became incredibly angry after finding out that she was travelling to Saint Croix with Rob, saying "The night before or sometime before, he had been out drinking and gotten drunk and apparently he was upset that he was not the one that was with Jennifer.

Zimmer would later remark that the ex-boyfriend was cleared by the police, saying "They talked with him several times, and while police say he is not a suspect in the case, certainly you get the feeling from others that he should be talked to a little bit more."

Current Boyfriend

Jennifer's boyfriend, Rob, was initially considered a suspect in her disappearance. The couple had just returned from a vacation in Saint Croix, in the U.S. Virgin Islands, and Rob was the last person who had spoken with Jennifer the night before her disappearance. Police soon interviewed Rob to learn more about his relationship with Jennifer and to ascertain his whereabouts the morning of her disappearance.

However, Rob was quickly discounted as a suspected. Rob had an airtight alibi; he was more than 200 miles away when Jennifer was abducted, at his home in Fort Lauderdale, Florida. Investigative journalist Beau Zimmer says, "The police said that between his phone records and the fact that he was in South Florida, we don't believe that he was involved."

The police department's belief in Rob's innocence is shared by Jennifer's family. He was fully cooperative with the police department and FBI's investigation and willingly provided a DNA sample twice. Jennifer's father, Drew Kesse, said "Rob has been put over the coals, Rob has been polygraphed three of four times, Rob has been interviewed probably over a dozen times."

Coworker

Both Jennifer's family, friends, and coworkers reported that Jennifer had recently turned down a coworker who was hitting on her and attempting to strike up a romantic relationship. Jennifer's mom, Joyce, said that the coworker was married and was refusing to accept Jennifer's decision not to date him, both because he was married and because she did not date people she worked with. Joyce later said, "Jennifer arranged to meet him in the cafeteria at work so that once and for all she could tell him, 'Leave me alone, I am never going to date you. And besides, I don't date married men.'"

The police department did question Jennifer's coworker and eventually eliminated him from the list of suspects. However, Joyce said "We feel it should have been consistent to keep the pressure on that individual."

Construction Workers

Jennifer, who had just purchased and moved into her newly renovated condo two months before her disappearance, had repeatedly expressed concern about construction workers in her complex. The complex, which was undergoing extensive renovations at the time, was housing undocumented immigrants working on the consecution projects, at the time of her disappearance. Beau Zimmer has stated, "Jennifer told some of her friends that she felt really uncomfortable around some of these guys. Apparently there may have been some cat calls and things like that."

Jennifer's parents have also stated that she may have been abducted by a construction worker, with her mother saying, "I can't help wonder if someone was stalking her from afar that she didn't even know. Could there have been someone watching her comings and goings?"

The local police department did question many of the construction workers who were working at her condo complex at the time of her disappearance; however, no leads would develop from this line of questioning. Zimmer would say, "The police tried to talk to as many of the workers that would have been there when Jennifer disappeared, but they acknowledge that they may have missed some people."

Sex Traffickers

Drew Kesse has claimed that it is well-known that there was an active sex trafficking ring in the Orlando area at the time of Jennifer's disappearance, which her parents think may be linked to her abduction. Jennifer's father, Drew Kesse, has stated "My gut feeling to this day, honestly, I truly believe she was trafficked." His sentiment was echoed by Jennifer's close friend and local television reporter Scott Thuman, was said "It would make sense on a lot of levels, as unfortunate as it is."

Reaction

The disappearance of Jennifer Kesse led to nationwide outrage and attention, with coverage in the local, state, national, and international media. At the behest of Orlando Police Department chief Val Demings, the FBI took over control of the case on June 10, 2010 and remains in-charge of her missing persons case to this day. She remains on the FBI's Missing List and they continue to search for her and react to current leads, with the most recent search taking place in February 2014. She is also still considered still missing by the Orlando Police Department, Interpol, and the Orange County, Florida Police Department.

In reaction to Jennifer's disappearance and the investigation into her disappearance. The Florida House of Representatives passed Senate Bill 502, entitled "The Jennifer Kesse and Tiffany Sessions Missing Persons Act," by unanimous vote on May 2, 2008. This bill changed the way that missing persons cases are handled in the state of Florida, instituting reforms such as allowing the Florida Department of Law Enforcement to provide assistance in missing persons cases involving adults. Prior to the passage of this law, the FDLE was limited in its ability to provide assistance in cases involving the disappearance or abduction of adults aged 26 or older.

THE DISAPPEAR-
ANCE OF TARA
CALICO

NICK PESCI

Tara Calico Mystery

The story of Tara Calico is one of confusion, uncertainty, and sadness. The events of her disappearance are one of the least understood of any crime over the past 50 years. A single Polaroid showing what is widely believed to be Tara, ultimately gives her disappearance its most notable name: The Polaroid Mystery.

Tara Calico was born on February 28, 1969 to loving parents in New Mexico. She led the typical American childhood. She had a huge amount of friends and extended family. Many were drawn to her bright personality and contagious smile. Even at an early age, she was developing into a tall, athletic young woman. She took a great interest in sports and outdoor activities. Among her favorite things to do was biking, hiking, and camping.

Tara Calico succeeded greatly in school. She had a strong interest in most every subject. Her parents would describe her as "the sweetest girl who never wanted to get in trouble". She had earned an opportunity to continue her education at the University of New Mexico at Valencia.

She had also formed a strong relationship with her boyfriend around the time she turned 18 years old. The two were seemingly a perfect match. Instead of movies and dinners, this couple preferred biking and walking, most any activity that required physical activity. Tara's parents enjoyed seeing her so happy. When she was just 19 years old, however, things would change forever.

On the morning of September 20, 1988 everything would change for Tara and her family. She was in a joyful mood. She was enjoying a day off from school at her family home in Belen, New Mexico. The weather was perfect. It was a mild morning and a great climate to get out and enjoy the day. Tara was an avid biker. She decided to embark on a long, 17 mile bike route that would ultimately lead to her returning back to her home in Belen.

She planned to leave at 9:30 A.M. The route she would take would make an elaborate oval that would take her around the railroad tracks as well as the Rio Communities

Golf Course. The route had some definite scenic areas, especially the trail along the railroad tracks. The beautiful weather meant that she would be able to make great time on the trip.

She had a lunch date with her boyfriend for noon. The couple planned to play tennis that afternoon. She had made a phone call to her boyfriend that morning and everything was completely normal. Looking back at the entire event, there was one thing that eerily stood out to her family. Before Tara left for her bike ride, she had told her mother jokingly that "if she wasn't back by noon, to come look for her." This was meant to be a playful banter between Tara and her mother, but ultimately could not have been any truer. This was the ultimate, real life foreshadowing that would turn out to be such a nightmare for all involved. Upon leaving for her bike ride at 9:30 A.M. she made her statement and rode off into the gorgeous morning air. This would be the last time anyone would see her alive in person.

Noon approached, and passed. Tara's mother became a bit anxious at the whole situation. Specifically, Tara was not one to arrive late or not show up when she was supposed to. All her mother could think of was the grim last words she had been told by Tara. As 12:30 P.M. approached, Patty Doel, Tara's mother, decided to look along the route she had taken to quell her worries. At this point, Patty felt it was likely that Tara was just running behind or maybe even stopped to enjoy the beautiful day. All that being said, Patty got in her car and went out to search along the route.

Patty got in her car and headed south on N.M. 47. This led to the Rio Communities where she would spend the majority of her trek. Seeing no sign of Tara in the least, full panic began to set in for Patty. Perhaps she had taken an alternate route or had merely stopped to see a friend. As it approached 1:00 P.M. Patty knew something was wrong. A strong sense of uneasiness came over Patty Doel. Something just wasn't right. By this time, she had missed her tennis date with her boyfriend and was entirely too late to assume that she had just been riding at a slow pace. Tara was a teenager who rode her bike religiously. A 17 mile ride would not take near this long, especially with a known route that she had used many times before. Something was terribly wrong, and it was up to Patty to figure out what that may be.

Patty continued to circle the roads around the Rio Communities. She decided it may be best to creep along the shoulder of the road in an attempt to see into the ditches. Maybe Tara had an accident and was stuck in the ditch. What Patty would find would confirm her worst fear.

Patty Doel froze as she saw something laying on the side of the road. It was a Boston cassette tape.

Tara Calico was a typical teenage girl for the time as she loved music. She was a huge fan of Boston. Most any bike ride that Tara would take would feature a water bottle, helmet, and her Sony Walkman. Most often, she would be listening to Boston.

The morning of September 20 was no different. She had her water bottle, helmet, and her Sony Walkman. She had a Boston cassette tape to accompany her on her long bike ride that morning.

As Patty approached the cassette tape and noticed that it was Boston, she lost all control of her worries. She knew in her heart that something was terribly wrong. Patty Doel immediately called police.

An expansive search of the area followed. Police questioned her family to get a sense of any possible place she could have went. Investigators initially believed that she was likely at a friend's house and failed to notify her mother. After all, she was a 19 year old college student. She easily could have felt that it was not necessary to notify her mother of minor changes to her day like this. Patty knew better. Patty suspected foul play. She also felt that Tara was smart enough to have left the Boston cassette as a clue to investigators and her mother that something wasn't right.

All those that were interviewed agreed that Tara was

not the kind to vanish without notifying those around her. She had never done anything like that before, and she had no reason to have done it then. Her boyfriend agreed, citing that she had never missed a date they had scheduled and would never "stand him up", especially for an activity such as tennis or anything else physical. At this point, full panic mode had been reached by everyone who was at all close to Tara. It was now a race against the clock.

At this point, police were quite skeptical of the entire situation. A Boston cassette on the side of the road and a 19 year old woman who was late returning home was, in their mind, just simply not enough to conduct a full missing person report. After all, there were thousands of Boston cassette, presumably, in the area. If a missing person report and search was filed each time a 19 year old was late coming home, then there would be hundreds of such reports each day.

Everything changed for police later that day. A policeman spotted a pink Huffy bicycle in a ditch along with a Sony Walkman roughly 20 miles from the home of Tara Calico. This changed everything. Police were now as convinced as Tara's family that something substantial had happened to her. Her bicycle, Walkman, and Boston cassette found thrown in the ditch caught their attention. Moreover, the location of the bicycle being so far from the home alerted police that she had either been taken from this location, or perhaps had been taken closer to her home and the bike and Walkman were simply thrown out at this point. Either way, investigators knew they had a major problem on their hands. They also knew that time was of utter importance if there was any hope to find Tara alive. They would need to work fast and efficiently.

    New Mexico detectives began to put all of their resources to this case. They questioned anyone around the seen and interviewed hundreds of people. Being as the route that Tara was to take was so long, they felt confident that someone, somewhere saw something of importance that may lead to a break in the case. Several people confirmed that a 1953 Ford F-150 pickup truck had been seen following Tara just a few miles from her house. This truck had an attached camper shell on it, which would prove significant. It was not known if Tara Calico knew who these people were, or even if she was aware someone was behind her. After all, she had music blaring in her ears from her Walkman which likely would have made it impossible for her to hear anything behind her.

Investigators felt it was significant to understand a bit about the social aspect of Tara. Tara Calico was a tall, athletic young woman who anyone would say was an attractive woman. There were many men who wanted to be with her and date her, and she was vocal to her friends about how she was approached many times by men asking her out. Her boyfriend affirmed this, as he said men had even approached her when they were together. Investigators thought this was significant for two reasons. First, Tara may very well have known who these people were. If she knew who was in the F-150, she may have simply been ignoring them and continuing on her route. Second, Tara may not have understood the present danger by strangers approaching her. After all, she had been approached on numerous occasions by strangers and may have just chalked it up to another guy trying to get a date with her. All in all, police could neither prove nor support these theories without more evidence. Finding a motive or a reason in an effort to gain a lead would prove near impossible.

    Even with extensive investigation by New Mexico police, the case really had no lead. The 1953 Ford F-150 was searched for in the area. However, it was not found. Tara Calico was proven to be on the bike trails and the streets around the trails on her 17 mile route. It was also confirmed that her bike and Sony Walkman were those that were found by police on the day of her disappearance. With eye witness testimony and her last known activity before her disappearance, police had nothing at all to work on for the case. She had seemingly disappeared without a trace beyond her bike and Walkman. The case ran cold for almost a year. Posters were put out, local news showed her picture and garnered attention to a hotline number for information on whereabouts. Family members urged anyone who knew anything suspicious to come forward. Rewards were offered by police and family members alike. There just weren't any leads in the case. Life would drag along for the family of Tara and her boyfriend, who was actually a suspect early in the case as police searched for answers. The whole situation was a sad reminder that closure may not come in this case, and that Tara may never be found alive. What started as a beautiful day that was perfect for a bike ride, turned into the worst nightmare for all of those involved. Police, however, finally caught a break in the most unlikely of cases. What would be discovered would be the single piece of evidence that would put this case on a national stage, and would ultimately give the case its name.

As the months dragged on, few within the family of Tara Calico thought any answers would arrive. In June of

1989, a break in the case would come. The harsh reality of this break, however, was that it would bring about many more questions with fewer answers.

It was a blistering summer for most all of the United States. In Port St. Joe, Florida, the heat was at an extreme. In this unlikely place, the name of Tara Calico would be brought to the forefront.

Port St. Joe Florida is just over 1,600 miles away from Belen, New Mexico. The story of Tara Calico had been scarcely seen in this distant place. On a June afternoon, nearly 9 full months since Tara Calico disappeared from Belen, New Mexico, a woman came upon something on the ground in a grocery store parking lot that caught her eye. As she walked closer to the strange object laying on the ground, she discovered it to be a single Polaroid photograph. This obviously peaked her curiosity. She decided that she would pick this photograph up. The striking image she would discover would open the case of Tara Calico up in a way never imagined.

The photograph showed a grave image. There were two people in the photograph. One of the people was a teenage woman, the other, a young boy, perhaps around ten years old. Both of them had black tape covering their mouths, not wrapped all the way around the head but just about ear to ear across the mouth. Each of them had their hands seemingly tied behind their backs, although the hands are out of picture so any further information on this is solely based on assumption. The woman is tall, having very long legs and a slight discoloration on the right calf, appearing to be a scar of some sort. She is wearing black gym style shorts with a grey t-shirt. She has dark colored hair that is pulled back behind her head. Nearly her whole body is visible in the photograph. The boy is in the background angle of the photograph. He is much younger than the female in the picture, and he too has black tape over his mouth in the same manner. His hands are also behind his back, assumed to be tied up. He is wearing a light blue t-shirt.

The face of each of them tell a story. The look of fear is much more present on the young boys face. They look tired and confused and are both staring directly at the camera.

The photo appears to have been taken in the back of a van of some sort. Both of the apprehended people are on blankets and pillows lying down with their heads against the side of the structure. The background is dark, creating an image that appears to have no light directly in their area, rather light that is coming in from the front of the structure behind the person taking the photograph.

In the bottom left corner of the photograph is a book. The book titled *My Sweet Andria* was written by V.C. Andrews. This would prove to be a key clue to investigators.

The woman quickly turned in the photograph to authorities. Upon investigation of the area, witnesses reported that a white Toyota cargo van had been parked in the area that morning. The van nor the driver were ever located. Witnesses described the driver of the van to be in his 30's with a thick handlebar style mustache. He was reported to be slender and of extremely fair complexion. He would never be located officially by investigators.

Investigators quickly noticed a striking resemblance to Tara Calico. Patty Doel was brought in to study the photograph and was convinced that it was Tara. Upon close review and a bit of background on Tara, she had strong reason to believe so.

The woman in the Polaroid was tall, athletic, and very slender toned. This matched Tara exactly. The hair color matched as well as the facial features and shape. The scar on the right leg of the woman in the photograph was also a chilling resemblance to one that Tara had. These clues in themselves were enough to safely attest that the girl in the photograph was, in fact, Tara Calico.

In addition to the physical features of the woman in the photograph was the odd placement of the book next to her. The book was written by V.C. Andrews, which was oddly enough the favorite author of Tara. She had read all of the V.C. Andrews books and was an avid reader. This, to many investigators and to Patty Doel, was the final piece of evidence to prove that the woman in the photograph was Tara Calico. But who was the boy in the photograph?

The young boy in the Polaroid appeared to be between 9 and 11 years old. Investigators initially believed the young boy to be Michael Henley. Michael went missing in April of 1988 in Zunis Mountain, New Mexico. He was camping with his family when he wandered off and never returned to the campsite. This would make the most sense to investigators as is would explain why Tara Calico was in the photograph as well. Both of the victims would have been assumed to have been taken from the same area around the same time.

In 1990, however, Michael Henley's remains were found just a few miles from the area that the family had been camping. It was determined that he died from exposure to the elements after presumably becoming lost in the wilderness of the area and not being able to find his way back. This was a turning point in the case as it raised doubts in the investigators minds as to the true identity of the people in the photograph.

Another problem that investigators had with the photograph was the legitimacy of the photo itself. Several people claimed that the Polaroid appeared staged. While this is a grim thought that is a terrible thing to assume, it was in fact a reality of the times. Singer Marilyn Manson famously set photos similar to this out randomly in this area as a prank. Most investigators, however, felt this photo was legitimate and not in any way staged.

Joel Nugent believed the photo to be entirely genuine. Joel Nugent was the lead investigator of the Florida case as a part of the Gulf County Sheriff's Department.

"It obviously is two kids with terror written all over them. It's kind of a bad time when you have to look at something like that and wonder. No one knows for sure if the picture was a setup. Some people think it was a stage photograph, but it was a real look of fear for me."

On September 20, 1989 *Unsolved Mysteries* aired a special on the Tara Calico disappearance. It marked the one year anniversary of her disappearance. Months prior, in July 1989, a special on Tara was aired on *A Current Affair*. Additionally, as the months turned into years, and the years turned in to decades, the story of Tara Calico was shown to a National audience on several other venues including *48 hours* and *America's Most Wanted*. With all of the exposure came an influx of tips and leads for investigators to sort through. The case of the disappearance of Tara Calico remained unsolved with no credible leads. The investigation was entirely cold.

It was not until 2008, nearly 20 years since Tara had disappeared, that this case would return to the fore front of the media. Valencia County, New Mexico Sheriff Renee Rivera released a statement claiming that he knew exactly what had happened to Tara. The problem, however, that he indicated is that the body of Tara Calico had never been found. This would make it impossible to bring those responsible, or at least who he felt was responsible, to justice.

"The individuals who did harm to Tara knew who she was. They knew who she was, and they are all local individuals. And I believe that the parents of the attackers were some of the people that helped the individuals with hiding the truth or hiding the body or trying to escape persecution," Rivera said.

Rivera never gave the suspects names. Rivera did, however, give his belief on what happened to Tara. Sheriff Rivera claims that two teenagers, roughly the same age as Tara, were involved in the crime. He also believed that several of the men's family members helped to cover up the crime.

"You know it's very frustrating, being that there's a lot of people who know what happened," Rivera said. "They know the whereabouts of the body or the remains. I believe that the body is somewhere very close. The body is somewhere very nearby."

Rivera had been approached by many informants over the previous couple of years. The informants all shared similar stories to what really happened to Tara Calico. According to the informants and Renee Rivera's statements, Tara never made it more than a few miles from her house on September 20, 1989. She was struck by the two teenagers who were driving a pickup truck. Rather than alert authorities and handle the situation the right way, the boys told their families and the families helped to bury the body of Tara Calico. The informants attest that the intention was not to hit Tara Calico, but to approach her while she was on her bike.

"She was really pretty young girl. She was very athletic, and a lot of guys wanted to talk to her, they wanted to meet her, they wanted to go out with her. And while she was riding her bike, they went up to try to talk to her, try to grab her, whatever, while she was on the bike," Rivera said.

Many people have questioned the basis of Sheriff Rivera's claims. While the claims do make sense and would line up with the evidence that investigators had uncovered, why is it 20 years later that the Sheriff would come out and voice these claims. If Rivera had such strong reason to make these allegations and had informants that were willing to speak as to what happened, why has there been no conviction? This is a question that remains to be answered.

Sadly, in 2006, Patty Doel, the mother of Tara Calico, passed away. She dealt with such a heavy heart and severe burden since Tara's disappearance in 1989. She passed away never knowing the truth as to what happened to Tara on the fateful day. Tara's father passed away in 2002 as well. Tara Calico's family never recovered from that dreadful morning, and never got the answers they needed for any sort of effort of closure. Tara's family is still searching for the truth of the events of that day. Thanks to social media, there are thousands of people nationwide that have joined in to find any answers or leads that may result in the truth.

The identity of the boy in the photograph still remains a mystery as well. The fact that neither victim in the photograph has ever been fully confirmed or identified remains a great mystery. While most every investigator will attest that woman in the photograph is indeed Tara Calico, there is no way to match an identity without the actual DNA evidence.

The story of Tara Calico is undeniably tragic. The truth is largely unknown. There have been no arrest and no attempts at arrest in the years since the horrific disappearance. While many believe the overall story that Sheriff Rivera told as to what had really happened to Tara, there has been no attempts to convict anyone of the heinous crime. The only true fact of this case is that a promising future was cut short while she was enjoying a beautiful September day. Perhaps one day the mystery of

Tara Calico will be fully understood. Perhaps one day justice will come forth and healing can begin.

Made in the USA
Monee, IL
01 January 2021